The Mystery of the Triune God

To my mother, sister and brother,
my first family of faith
in the triune God

The Mystery
of the
Triune God

John J. O'Donnell

Paulist Press
New York/Mahwah

First published in Great Britain by Sheed & Ward Ltd.

Library of Congress Cataloging-in-Publication Data

O'Donnell, John J. (John Joseph), 1944–
    The mystery of the triune God / by John J. O'Donnell.
        p.   cm.
    Bibliography: p.
    Includes index.
    ISBN 0-8091-3112-9
    1. Trinity   2. Catholic Church—Doctrines.   I. Title.
    BT111.2.036   1990
    231'.044—dc20   89-32894
                                                                CIP

Published by Paulist Press
997 Macarthur Boulevard
Mahwah, New Jersey 07430

Printed and bound in the
United States of America

Contents

Preface

In the introduction to *Foundations of Christian Faith*, Karl Rahner asks himself the question: for whom has this book been written? This is the question which I have asked myself as this study gradually took shape. To answer the question, I think it is important to note that the book has arisen out of annual attempts to lecture on the doctrine of God at Heythrop College, University of London and at the Gregorian University, Rome. These lectures have prompted me to try to synthesize what I believe about God in a form which is understandable to students. Many theologians have acknowledged the fact that it is probably impossible today to write an entire Christian dogmatics. Otto Pesch argues that the best that one can hope to do is to present a synthesis of the individual tracts of dogmatic theology based on repeated attempts to lecture on a given thematic.[1] The results of this type of attempt are what I offer in this study. I have tried to cull the best insights of the tradition and of modern theology and to integrate them into a synthesis which respects the exigencies of the scholar and which is intelligible as well to students, pastors, catechists and educated adults who are interested in exploring the meaning of their faith in God. With Rahner, I can only say that I hope I will find readers for whom the book is neither too primitive nor too advanced.

A second desire has motivated me in preparing this text. One often hears today the lament that there is a terrible dichotomy between theology and life, between theology and spirituality. Theology is often accused of being spiritually barren. For this reason I have tried to present the Christian faith in the triune God not as a speculative treatise but as the scaffolding which undergirds not only Christian thinking about God but also Christian living and prayer. With this problematic in mind I have included the two chapters: 'Trinitarian Faith and Praxis' and 'Trinitarian Prayer'.

Finally, I should like to admit that the more I have reflected upon my faith in God and on the way in which theology should be done, the more value I believe must be attached to tradition. This book is written by one who thinks, lives and prays within the Roman Catholic tradition. This tradition has given me the theological air which I breathe. As a Catholic reflecting on this tradition, I have been fully committed to the Mystery of the triune God. That God is the triune Mystery, Father, Son and Holy Spirit, has never been a question. I recognize that there are theologians today for whom the doctrinal decisions of the early councils are questionable and open to revision. For some of them the confession of the Trinity as an ontological reality was a dubious historical decision which is reversible. As a Catholic I cannot accept such a view of tradition. As Karl Rahner has said, every dogmatic definition in one sense represents an end. But he went on to say that it also represents a beginning. For the living tradition of the faith of the church is a constant invitation to reflection. I hope that in this sense the present book represents an open Catholicism, which is ready to enter into dialogue with and to learn from other points of view.

I am grateful to Heythrop College and to the Gregorian University for giving me the forum to develop these ideas. And I would like to dedicate this book to my mother, brother and sister who were the first family in which the seed of my faith in God was planted and nurtured.

I

The Dilemma of Contemporary Thinking About God

This is a book about the Trinity. But in proposing to write about trinitarian theology I am not intending to write about one specialized problematic within Christian theology. Rather, in writing about the Trinity, I am writing about our Christian experience of God, for according to our faith, when we say that we believe in God, we mean by the word God, the Father, the Son and the Holy Spirit. Apart from this three-fold confession of faith, we have no experience of God. And thus for us Christians our experience of the Trinity and our belief in God stand or fall together.

This fact reminds us that the concept of God is by no means something which we can simply presuppose. One of the greatest difficulties of faith is to explain exactly what one means by God. This problem is reflected as early as the New Testament where St Paul writes (I Cor. 8):

> For although there may be so-called gods in heaven or on earth –
> as indeed there are many 'gods' and many 'lords' – yet for us
> there is one God, the Father, from whom are all things and for
> whom we exist, and one Lord, Jesus Christ, through whom are
> all things and through whom we exist. (vv. 5–6).

The same problematic is revealed at the beginning of St Thomas's *Summa Theologica*. At the beginning of this work Aquinas presents five arguments for the existence of God based on the philosophy of Aristotle. At the end of each proof Thomas concludes, 'And this everyone calls God.' Many of the difficulties which people today have with the five ways have less to do with the arguments themselves than with the conclusion. Do we in fact mean by God the unmoved mover, the first cause, the divine orderer of reality etc?

This raises the question of how we are to understand the relationship between the philosophical concept of God and the God of revelation. How do we relate the God of philosophy to the God of Christianity? As an illustration of this problematic, let us mention the problem of God's relation to history. In the Greek world perfection was associated with the transcendence of time and freedom from suffering. Aristotle's god, for example, is a changeless thought thinking itself. This concept has dramatically influenced the world in which Christianity first flourished. On the other hand, the Hebrew mentality associates God with historical events. Christianity goes even further, asserting that God has identified himself totally with a slice of history, namely the life of Jesus of Nazareth. God has become temporal in this man. Moreover, Christianity even dares to assert that God has identified himself with the suffering and with the cross of this man. Hence God and suffering are not contradictories. One of the supreme challenges for Christianity is to think God in union with temporality and in union with perishability.[1] But then the Christian understanding is bound to come into conflict with certain traditional ways of thinking about God. With these brief introductory remarks, let us look at some of the conundrums which result from the human effort to think about God. After having explored these paths, perhaps it will emerge that the experience of God in Jesus Christ offers us a new way to understand God.

The Antinomy of Theism

Let us consider for a moment the classical idea of God. In the philosophy of St Thomas, God is identified as the fullness of being. God is pure act. There is in him neither becoming nor potency and hence God cannot change, for change presupposes the transition from potency to act. When St Thomas considers God's relation to the world, he analyzes first of all the various types of relationships. There is, to begin with, a rational relationship which is one which exists only in the mind. Then there is a real relationship which implies that the relation is real in both members of the relation. For example, when I am having a conversation with another person, we are mutually affecting one another, receiving each other's communication and responding to one another. St Thomas mentions a third type of relation, a mixed relation in which the relation is real in only one member of the term. For example, if I am standing on one side of my desk and move to the other side, I have changed in relation to the desk but the desk has remained as it was. There is a mixed relation in that the relation is real only in myself, in one term of the relation. Aquinas explains that God's relation to the world is exactly his type of relation.[2] God never changes *vis-à-vis* the world, although the world is constantly changing in relation to him.

Aquinas understands this relation first of all in terms of God's creative activity. God, as the fullness of Being, is the efficient cause of everything which happens in the world. John Macquarrie has referred to this idea of the God-world relation as monarchic. There is no reciprocity of relations between God and the world. Everything flows from God to the world:

> The world needs God but God has no need of the world. God affects the world but the world does not affect God. The world owes everything to God but God is not increased by the world.[3]

The greatest difficulty about this whole conception of God is the religious implication which seems to follow from it. If the God-world relationship is always asymmetric, then it follows that God literally cannot be affected by anything which happens in the world. He is, for example, unaffected by the suffering of his creatures. Also this view strikes a blow at human freedom. The ultimate seriousness of my freedom is threatened, for in the last analysis it makes no difference to God whether I love him or not, whether I use my freedom for good or evil. It is extremely difficult to reconcile this picture of God with the biblical portrait of God who goes in search of men and women and rejoices when a lost son finds his way back to the house of his Father. The whole biblical story presupposes that God responds to human decisions and is affected by them. This serious religious objection against the classical doctrine of theism has led a number of modern theologians, even Thomists, to revise the idea of God in St Thomas. While not wholly willing to surrender the notion of God as the full plenitude of Being, the Thomistic philosopher Norris Clarke is prepared to admit that today we must speak of God as having a real relation to the world, and he even sees the need to revise our conception of God's immutability. Interestingly, the principal motive for Clarke is to make God more religiously available. He writes:

> Now if we are to take seriously the religious dimension of human experience ... then it is clear that one of the central tenets of man's religious belief in God (at least in Judaeo-Christian religion) is that He is one who enters into deep personal relations of love with his creatures. And an authentic interpersonal relation

3

of love necessarily involves not merely purely creative or one-way love, but genuine mutuality and reciprocity of love, including not only the giving of love but the joyful acceptance of it and response to it. This means that our God is a God who really cares, is really concerned with our lives and happiness, who enters into truly reciprocal personal relations with us, who responds to our prayers – to whom, in a word, our contingent world and its history somehow make a genuine difference.[4]

In the face of such difficulties, a number of modern philosophers have abandoned the traditional concept of God and substituted a God who is in the process of becoming along with the rest of reality. A well-known approach along these lines is that of Whitehead and Hartshorne. Whitehead wants to replace the category of being as the ultimate reality with that of becoming. Reality is as such a process, a dynamic becoming. In *Process and Reality*, Whitehead argues that the ultimate metaphysical category is that of creativity. Early in this work, he states the fundamental axiom which interprets all of reality. 'The many become one and are increased by one.'[5] Creativity is truly the ultimate in this system. In other words we cannot ask why there is a process of becoming. As philosophers we can only describe the nature of reality as we experience it. God therefore is not an ultimate explanation of reality. For Whitehead, God is a factor within the metaphysical situation. God does not decide the laws of reality but, as Whitehead observes, he is their ultimate exemplification.

It is difficult to exaggerate what a revolutionary view this is which Whitehead proposes. For example, he writes, 'Neither God, nor the World, reaches static completion. Both are in the grip of the ultimate metaphysical ground, the creative advance into novelty.'[6] Whitehead also states, 'In the philosophy of organism this ultimate is termed "creativity"; and God is its primordial, non-temporal accident.'[7]

Without going into the complexities of Whitehead's doctrine of God, it is fairly easy to see that his God lacks many of the perennial divine attributes. For example, God is temporal, passible, suffers with the world, is able to increase in his perfection as the world grows in novelty. Whitehead admits, for example, that he surrenders the classical notion of God's transcendence. For Whitehead,

God is both transcendent and immanent. God is transcendent in that he is eternal, and in his primordial nature contains the entire realm of possibilities for the world. But God is also non-transcendent in the sense that he cannot be God apart from the world. God is dependent on his creation. Having the infinite realm of potentialities in his primordial nature, there is a sense in which God is independent of creation, but for God to become concrete he has to realize some of these potentialities in interacting with the creation. There is an immense scope both for the freedom of God and the creation in this process of interaction but what is strictly necessary is that God relate himself to some world or other. Without such a relation God could never be more than an abstraction. The difficulty is whether such a limitation of God's transcendence is really justifiable philosophically or whether it is compatible with the Judaeo-Christian biblical understanding of God as creator. Contemporary process theologians are aware that they are surrendering (or drastically modifying) an important element of our Christian heritage. For example, *a propos* of the doctrine of creation, Whitehead writes:

> God can be termed the creator of each temporal actual entity. But the phrase is apt to be misleading by its suggestion that the ultimate creativity of the universe is to be ascribed to God's volition. The true metaphysical position is that God is the aboriginal instance of this creativity, and is therefore the aboriginal condition which qualifies its action. It is the function of actuality to characterize the creativity, and God is the eternal primordial character. But of course, there is no meaning to 'creativity' apart from its 'creatures', and no meaning to 'God' apart from the creativity and the 'temporal creatures', and no meaning to the temporal creatures apart from 'creativity' and 'God'.[8]

One might ask whether this approach of process theology does adequate justice to the classical affirmation that God is the One who creates out of nothing or even to our human experience of being creatures. Karl Rahner, for example, locates the doctrine of creation in our human experience of transcendence. Transcendence indicates that the human subject is a dynamic propulsion beyond himself toward the Absolute. For Rahner, human transcendence exists in two dimensions, that of knowledge and of freedom. Every human act of knowledge is profoundly finite. I know some object in the world. But in knowing an object the drive of my intellect is never satisfied. Each act of knowing in turn raises a new question. This questioning will never cease nor will it ever arrive at its goal. For Rahner, human knowing is thus situated between the finite and the infinite. Nothing is clearer than the finitude of human knowledge. But since knowing is not static but dynamic, it is paradoxically in the finite that I become aware of the infinite as the horizon, the 'whither' of my transcendence. The same could be said of freedom. In each act of choice I decide upon something finite in the world, but each act of freedom reveals the gap between what I have chosen and the dynamism of my subjectivity. Therefore human freedom also opens up to an infinite horizon. It is only within this horizon that my finite freedom is recognized as finite. Rahner would argue: (1) that human knowledge and freedom are finite and conditioned; (2) that this is true in every human act whatsoever; and (3) that precisely in acknowledging the limits of my finite knowledge and freedom, I am necessarily driven beyond my finitude to the infinite as the condition of possibility of my human transcendence. As I suggested above, this is a philosophical analysis of what in theological terms is meant by the doctrine of creation.

Proceeding along the same lines, Peter Knauer suggests the following definition of being a creature: a complete reference to, in a complete differentiation from, God.[9] As I have just indicated, in every act of knowing and willing, I am referred beyond myself to the transcendent. At the same time, I recognize my radical finitude. Precisely my reference beyond myself makes me realize the infinite gap between myself and God, hence the complete differentiation of God and the creature. The other important word here is 'complete', i.e. the reference beyond myself and the differentiation from God is total. It exists in every dimension of my being as a created reality. In other words there is nothing I can call my own. There is no ground on which I can stand and claim this as my own territory. In every dimension of my being whatsoever I am referred beyond myself. As Knauer says, take away the dimension of creatureliness and what is left is precisely nothing.

But paradoxically we notice that if one accepts this approach of Knauer and if one clings to the perennial affirmation of God as the

One who creates out of nothing (in the sense of: take away 'created-ness' and what is left is precisely nothing), one finds that one is back in the classical understanding of the God-world relation. The analysis of createdness which I have offered (following Rahner and Knauer) suggests a one-way relation between God and the world. The world is totally referred beyond itself to God but God is in no way referred to the world. We must say that we are related to God but cannot say that God has a real relation to us. This does indeed make sense in terms of preserving God's transcendence and human finitude. For, as Knauer points out, if God is essentially (i.e. of his very nature) referred to the world, this means that God and the world become part of a larger system. God becomes a piece of the world. God is reduced to the level of finitude. Or as Whitehead admits, God needs the world to be God. But then we are entitled to ask if God is really God, for God is no longer the ultimate, but rather there must be some other ultimate such as creativity of which God is the highest instantiation.

Are we then left with an antinomy? We have seen that the classical idea of God leads to serious religious difficulties in that God seems to be remote, indifferent to all that happens, unable to suffer or receive us into his life. On the other hand, some modern approaches to God such as that of Whitehead seem to so circumscribe the transcendence of God that God is no longer God. Is there no way out of this dilemma? Perhaps we must find the key in the wonder of revelation, for it would seem indeed that what God has shown us in his revelation is that he wants to be in a real relation to us. But before exploring this further, let us look again at another dilemma from which modern thinking about God finds it difficult to extricate itself.

Antinomy of the Classical Idea of God in Modern Philosophy

It is usually asserted that medieval philosophy is cosmocentric. For example, in St Thomas's epistemology, knowledge takes place when the world impinges itself on me. The first level of human knowledge is receptive. There is an intentionality of the world toward the human subject. In a second step the human mind is active, producing concepts and referring these concepts back to the world in the act of judgement. Thus according to Thomistic epistemology there is a double intentionality: of the world to the subject and of the subject to the world.

With Descartes, however, a change of perspective takes place which is determinative for the whole of modern philosophy. This shift is known as the anthropocentric turn. Now the human subject stands in the centre of reality and of philosophy. Philosophy becomes anthropocentric. According to this approach to philosophy, what I know is first of all conditioned by the kinds of questions I pose to reality. It is impossible to speak of sheer objective reality. Objects are always objects for subjects.

Descartes is a prime example of this new attitude. The whole of his philosophy is a search for certitude.[10] Descartes looks for an archimedian point on which he can build a secure edifice of knowledge. This he finds in the 'I think'. He is certain of himself as a thinking subject every time he pronounces his 'Cogito, ergo sum.' However, Descartes perceives that there is a problem of the continuity of certainty, for he has absolute certainty only in the atomistic moments of pronouncing his 'I think'. Then there is the problem of deception. Suppose there is an evil genius (which is really a double of the human intellect) who deceives me. Descartes brings in the idea of God at this point to overcome his doubt. If there is a God and if this God is true and good, then I have no need to fear the deception of the evil genius. In this perspective, Descartes introduces his ontological proof for the existence of God.

First of all, it is important to notice here that the place of God in Descartes's system is functional. God is not interesting for his own sake. God is brought in to bolster the human subject and guarantee his search for security. Already the notion of God is relativized.

Something pernicious is beginning to happen here, the full effects of which will not be seen for another century or two. According to Descartes, God's existence is known only when the subject utters the 'Cogito, ergo sum.' Hence God's existence is subtly made to depend on human consciousness. God is made to depend on human subjectivity. The full consequences of this are perceived by Feuerbach when he argues that God is really a superfluous extra of human subjectivity. There is no such thing as the infinite but God is another way of describing the infinity of consciousness itself.

The full ramifications of this shift of perspective from medieval theology can be seen in the classical distinction between the existence and essence of God. In any finite being there is a real distinction between essence and existence. For example, I exist as a human person but I could equally not exist. My act of existence is finite and limited. St Thomas would say that it is limited precisely by the essence of being human. In the case of God there is a real identity of essence and existence. The essence of God is to exist. As Thomas Aquinas says, God is 'Ipsum Esse Subsistens'. We can only make a rational distinction between his essence and existence. There is a distinction as far as our minds are concerned but no real distinction in God himself.

But, as Jüngel argues, the move which Descartes made, introduces a totally new perspective. Also for Descartes, God's existence and essence are identical. Descartes also wants to reach a being who cannot not exist. But by relativizing the existence of God, so that his existence is made proportionate to the existence of the 'I think' the human subject interposes himself between God's essence and existence. Jüngel sums up the fatal flaw of Descartes's strategy:

> The veiled problem consists in this, that God only attains the presence which lets him *be*, insofar as he is *thought of as God*. The ego as the res cogitans has become the subject of all existence. That means: certainly with respect to his *essence* God must be *above* me with himself and only with himself, even when he is thought of by me *as God*. But as this essence, God must, with respect to his *existence*, be present *with me and only with me*, because *through me*. Therefore, even while he is *thought of* as creator necessarily existing through himself, God is made into an object ... through the thinking subject. This is at any rate a contradiction which undermines God's Being: by making him into a supreme being above me *whose existence is through me and with me*.[11]

The conclusion of Jüngel's reasoning is that the whole project of Descartes which is carried through consistently in the course of modern philosophy has an in-built tendency to atheism. The splintering of the existence and essence of God through the mediation of the 'I think' makes God ultimately unthinkable and one is left in the end simply with the fact of human subjectivity alone.

Jüngel's treatment of Descartes is meant to demonstrate that the attempt to link the classical idea of God to human subjectivity is bound to fail and that the story of modern philosophy is the tale of this failure. In other words, in the whole project of modern philosophy, centred on the human subject, there is implicitly a methodological will to atheism. Jüngel makes an extensive and profound defence of this thesis with reference to a whole range of modern philosophers. Without reproducing those discussions here, it would be at least worthwhile to take note of one final point. Referring again to the classical idea of God, Jüngel draws our attention to the definition of God according to St Anselm.[12] God is that being a greater than which cannot be conceived. This implies, first of all, that the concept of God is the greatest achievement of the human mind. At the same time, Anselm wants to demonstrate that God is greater than the human mind. According to Anselm God's existence is not dependent on the human mind, for the greatest possible being is one who could not not exist. But hence, there is here a paradox. The supreme achievement of the human mind is *above* the human mind. In other words, as soon as I conceive this idea of God, I conceive of a God who is Lord above and over me. Hence as soon as I conceive God (my supreme achievement), I recognize myself as a creature, as not God. I see myself as therefore excluded from God. God is above and I am below. The human being's greatest achievement is to conceive a supreme being from which he is excluded. It is not difficult to see that there is only a short step from the separation of God and man (based on the concept of God) to the opposition of God and man. God becomes a threat to my humanity. Isn't this just the charge which so many modern atheists make against God? In Nietzsche's words, 'If there were gods, how could I endure it to be no god? *Therefore* there are no gods.'[13] This is substantially the same charge which the Marxist philosopher Ernst Bloch makes against theism. He speaks of God as 'an above, where no man exists.' For modern philosophers such as Bloch the classical idea of God as the supreme being necessarily excludes the human.[14] Therefore they reject theism in the name of humanism.

Reflecting then on classical theism and its idea of God in the light of modern philosophy, we are led to ask again if this understanding of God lands us in antinomies from which it is impossible to free ourselves. Does the classical understanding of God as it has been appropriated by modern philosophy itself have an in-built tendency to atheism? Is the concept of God in theism the only way to think God? Do we mean by God the supreme Being, opposed to time, change and suffering, a being from whom *per definitionem* the human is excluded, or, on the basis of revelation, is the challenge precisely to think God in union with humanity, with time and with perishability?

The Antinomies of Atheism

In the light of the conundrums involved in the classical idea of God, one might be led to believe that atheism is the only alternative. And in fact it is the case that contemporary atheism is in large measure a rejection of a specific tradition. As Jüngel argues, atheism is itself an historical phenomenon which must be understood historically.

Naturally the contemporary phenomenon of atheism is extremely complex. But for our purposes here we can consider briefly two forms of contemporary atheistic experience: atheism in the name of freedom and protest atheism against the situation of human suffering.

(1) Atheism in the name of freedom.

We have seen that the classical idea of a perfect God above seems to exclude the human. Therefore theism is often rejected as a form of heteronomy. God is over against man, imposing on him alien norms, standards and laws which restrict human freedom. The atheist often grounds his position in the desire for human autonomy. God is rejected in a postulatory way, so that man can be his own God, fashion the project of his own life and create his own norms on the basis of his own freedom.

This humanistic form of atheism can at first seem attractive but deeper reflection makes us aware that atheism also involves the human being in seemingly inextricable dilemmas. Kasper in *The God of Jesus Christ* has shown that the human being's understanding of self since the Enlightenment can be seen as a relentless quest for human freedom. And Kasper discerns at least two types of aspiration for freedom: the evolutionary and the revolutionary.[15] According to the evolutionary model of the Enlightenment, the human being is seen as a child who has now come of age. He no longer needs to live under the tutelage of religion with its authority, doctrines and norms. The mature human being can look to the sciences to provide him with a vision of life. Theology can be replaced with anthropology. Human destiny can be discerned through the discoveries of biology and physics, sociology and psychology. But two hundred years of the development of the natural sciences has revealed that these empirical disciplines do not answer the deeper questions which torture the human spirit, questions such as the meaning of life, of fate, of guilt, of suffering and death, of tragedy. Moreover, thinkers such as Horkheimer and Adorno of the Frankfurt School have shown that the so-called thinking of the Enlightenment involves a dialectic which is often enslaving. Enlightenment thinking is so functional that the human being becomes caught in a vicious circle of means and ends in which the value of the person is reduced to functionalism. The mentality of the Enlightenment is so pervasive that a whole culture has been created on the basis of a divinized technology which dehumanizes the person. Today our world bears abundant witness to the fact that technology, far from solving all the problems of human life and far from liberating the human being, creates new problems and enslaves the person to a degree unimaginable in the history of our ancestors. One has only to think of environmental problems, problems of diet and drugs or the technological advances in weaponry to see the vicious circle of destruction in which the Enlightenment mentality has involved us.

The other type of aspiration for freedom has been a revolutionary one. Perhaps this aspiration is embodied most clearly in Marx's call to the slaves and the oppressed of the world to throw off the shackles of slavery and rise up in an armed struggle against their oppressors. One only has to look at the various revolutionary movements throughout the world today from Nicaragua and South Africa to Iran and the Middle East to see how actual this interpretation of freedom is. However, even this revolutionary freedom seems to end in disappointment and failure. Some years ago in a masterly study of revolution, the philosopher Hannah Arendt raised the question how one can prevent the revolutionaries from devouring their own children.[16] In almost every instance of revolution, the protagonists, when they come to power, soon impose a new form of dictatorship with repression of liberties and censorship, all in the name of the people. Over one hundred years of revolution raise the disturbing question whether and how it is possible really to make a new beginning for freedom. Or is the human situation such that human freedom is really in bondage to an alien power and that all attempts to initiate freedom are bound to end in the vicious circle of slavery?

If looking at human freedom purely from below does not offer a satisfactory vision of human destiny, perhaps this does not mean that we must despair of realizing a free world. Perhaps the true nature of the situation is that human reality is always ambiguous, a mixture of freedom and limitation, liberty and bondage. But from this point of view, perhaps Kasper is correct in seeking that even the desire for liberty has a religious root.[17] In each human act of freedom the human subject is expressing his or her transcendence, albeit in a fragmentary and partial way. But nevertheless as an act of transcendence, freedom always anticipates the total freedom for which the person longs and which he knows at least implicitly as the goal of his finite transcendence. Freedom in this sense raises a religious question. Is there a kingdom of freedom or is the nature of reality ultimately blind, deterministic, mechanistic? Kant had a profound insight, when he saw that human freedom is possible only within a free universe. Unless freedom characterizes every level of reality, it is impossible for the human subject ultimately to be free.

As I say, looking at the aspiration for freedom from below, one sees perhaps only an antinomy. One sees two poles, both of which offer an antinomy. There is the hopeless choice between theism leading to heteronomy and atheism leading to autonomy. Heteronomy leaves one with an alien set of norms and values. But the autonomy of atheism leaves the human being, as Sartre so vividly perceived, a useless passion. Humankind is left in an indifferent universe having to bear the lonely burden of freedom in solipsistic anguish. But perhaps this dilemma suggests that a third version of freedom exists, a theonomous freedom in which the freedom of God and men and women are not in inverse but in direct proportion. But if such a freedom exists, it must be discovered as a gift, as the free offer of the God of revelation. Such freedom cannot be the postulate of human subjectivity. If it is genuine freedom, it must be a freedom freely offered and freely appropriated. Philosophy alone cannot decide whether such a freedom exists, but philosophical reflection upon experience can point to the question in human experience to which the Christian gospel offers a response. More-

over the Kantian intuition about the kingdom of freedom can alert us to a more perceptive reading of the gospel, for as Kasper notes, however strange the language of the Bible may appear, Jesus's message of the coming of the Kingdom of God, can be understood adequately, not as a religious message in itself, but only within the context of the human search for peace, freedom, justice and life.[18]
(2) Protest atheism against the situation of human suffering.

In addition to atheism in the name of human freedom, one of the most significant forms of contemporary atheism is the protest atheism which is based on the experience of human suffering. According to such atheists the greatest obstacle to belief is life itself. Human life reveals so much exploitation, oppression, persecution, injustice, violation of innocent victims, sickness and death, that it is difficult to believe in an all-good and all-powerful God, especially in one who is interested in the tragic state of human affairs. Therefore someone like Camus says that he cannot believe in a God while living in a world in which innocent children suffer and die. Instead Camus offers a modern version of stoicism, a philosophy of rebellion in which one struggles resolutely with the victims against all forces of death and destruction. According to this vision of reality, it is not so much God who is the problem but the world. This was also the point of view of Ivan in Dostoevsky's *The Brothers Karamazov*. If God created such a world, it would be better to hand back one's entrance ticket to life. Moltmann has said that the problem with the classical arguments for the existence of God is not the logic of the argument but the premises. For according to the classical proofs one proceeds from the experience of an ordered, contingent world, i.e. a cosmos, to the supreme being. But Moltmann contends that we do not find a cosmos. Living in a world of chaos, can we conclude to the existence of God or should we rather deduce the existence of a monster?[19]

Nevertheless the stoic alternative which many modern atheists offer is itself problematic. Certainly it is a tragic vision of life. The human being is hardly seen as a Promethean figure stealing fire from the gods. Rather, as Camus envisions him, he is more like Sisyphus rolling the stone up the mountain, only to watch it plummet to the earth again. At this moment he is summoned to take up the struggle anew. Moltmann, reflecting on this type of atheism, observes that the Achilles's heel of this protest is the inevitable drift toward resignation. One's freedom is bought at the price of despair:

The protesting atheist loves in a desperate way. He suffers because he loves, yet he protests against suffering and against love and easily becomes hardened. Like Ivan Karamazov, he wants to give back his admission ticket to life.[20]

Nevertheless, even in this protest atheism, we can see perhaps a religious dimension. Ernst Bloch has shown that much of the religious inspiration is based on human messianic desires and dreams. The key formula for interpreting the human is: S is not yet P. The human being in other words is not static. He is transcendence, always moving beyond himself. The goal toward which he is moving is utopia. The great religions such as Judaism and Christianity are responses to the human messianic drive. But this dynamism toward utopia is all the more urgent because of human suffering. Because he lives in a world of suffering and injustice, the human being in his transcendence experiences an insatiable desire for the peaceable kingdom. Another German philosopher, M. Horkheimer, has pointed to the same phenomenon and has observed that the human being is 'the search for the totally other.'[21] He is searching for a realm of perfect justice and righteousness, but no human situation ever adequately matches this dream. Even though Horkheimer is an atheist, he understands the anthropological foundation for the religions. Like Bloch he recognizes that the religions will not disappear, for they answer an irrepressible longing in the human heart. And Horkheimer also acknowledges that if such a utopia were to exist, it would have to include something like the resurrection of the dead. Only in a kingdom in which the dead are raised could there be a complete reconciliation of humankind with the world, a reconciliation in which the oppressor would no longer finally and ultimately triumph over his victim. But Horkheimer also recognizes that such a kingdom is a utopia. It would require a new creation, an absolutely new beginning, for within the present world, we are caught in a vicious circle of hatred, violence and revenge.

Conclusion

In this chapter we have tried to raise the question of what one means when one uses the word 'God' and we have reflected upon various dilemmas which result when one tries to think God. We began with the classical concept of God in theism and we indicated that this concept involves serious problems for a believer. Moreover, we have seen that the antinomies in this way of thinking about God have contributed to the situation of widespread atheism. Reflecting then upon atheism, we saw that this vision of life, although doing justice to a vast dimension of human experiences, also implies consequences which offer a less than satisfying vision of human life. At this point, we must ask ourselves if we have arrived at a cul-de-sac or is there a way forward. A number of modern authors such as Moltmann and Jüngel have suggested that the Christian idea of God must be seen precisely as a response to this impasse.[22] For such authors both theism and atheism are false attempts to think God. And as Moltmann points out, there is a common bond between them. Both have the idea of God as the perfect being, aloof from history, atemporal and impassible. Theism defends this concept of God; atheism rejects it. But certainly, *prima facie*, the Christian experience of God seems to be oriented in a different direction. For the source of Christian thinking about God is God's identification of himself with a particular slice of human time, namely the history of Jesus of Nazareth. Christian faith has always wanted to say that this history is God's own history. Surely that is the meaning of the incarnation. But when we look at this history, we notice something even more astounding. The history of Jesus culminates in the cross, i.e. in suffering and death. For us Christians, therefore, God and death are not contradictories, for the cross-event is for us a God-event. The precise challenge, therefore, of Christian thinking about God, is, as Jüngel stresses, to think God in unity with time and with perishing. The question then toward which our further reflections must be directed is this: what is there in God's self-revelation in Jesus Christ that makes us think of God in a new way and why is it that for Christianity this new way is thoroughly trinitarian, so that the content of the word 'God' is known to be Father, Son and Holy Spirit?

II

Revelation and Trinity

Anyone reflecting on the mystery of God today within the tradition of Catholic theology will have to take into account two major developments. The first is the shift of perspective as regards the church's understanding of revelation which took place between Vatican I and Vatican II. The second is the reopening of the question of the Trinity within Protestant theology since the time of Karl Barth. Let us begin by reflecting for a moment on these two developments. It is commonly asserted that Vatican I worked with a propositional view of revelation. God is said to reveal things about himself and about the destiny of men and women, which so transcend the grasp of the human mind that if God had not revealed them, they would be inaccessible to us. Thus according to Vatican I, there are two orders of knowledge, that based on faith and that based on reason. In its Constitution on faith *Dei Filius*, the council states:

> There are two orders of knowledge, distinct not only in origin but also in object. They are distinct in origin, because in one we know by means of natural reason; in the other, by means of divine faith. And they are distinct in object, because in addition to what natural reason can attain, we have proposed to us as objects of belief mysteries that are hidden in God and which, unless divinely revealed, can never be known.[1]

It is worth noting that in this text and elsewhere the council speaks of mysteries in the plural. It does the same when it speaks of the communication of divine truths. And it explains that these are mysteries properly so called because, of their very nature, they excel the power of the created intellect to understand them. Since they are beyond the grasp of our reason, the council offers as the ground of belief the extrinsic motive of the authority of the revealing God who can neither deceive nor be deceived.

By contrast, the Second Vatican Council works with a more profound concept of revelation, one which is thoroughly christological. In *Dei Verbum*, the council fathers abandoned the propositional model of revelation in favour of the model of self-disclosure. God does not so much reveal truths about himself or the mysteries of his being but rather he reveals or discloses himself. Thus the *Constitution on Divine Revelation* (no. 2) begins, 'In his goodness and wisdom, God chose to reveal Himself and to make known to us the hidden purpose of his will.' It is striking that in the same paragraph the council accentuates the soteriological significance of revelation, again using the singular rather than the plural for the truth of what God reveals. 'By this revelation then, the deepest truth about God and the salvation of man is made clear to us in Christ, who is the Mediator and at the same time the fullness of all revelation.' In this same sentence we see how the Second Vatican Council thinks of revelation in christological terms. Revelation is no longer seen as in Vatican I, in contrast to reason, but is oriented to history. We must look to the concrete historical events of space and time, i.e. to the history of Jesus of Nazareth, to discover the presence of God's revelation. *Dei Verbum* (no. 4) expresses this succinctly:

> For this reason Jesus perfected revelation by fulfilling it through his whole work of making himself present and manifesting himself: through his words and deeds, his signs and wonders, but especially through his death and glorious resurrection from the dead and final sending of the Spirit of truth.

Already in these brief passages the council hints at the fact that the Christian revelation can only be understood adequately in trinitarian terms. For the point of the affirmations in no. 2 is that God the Father reveals and makes himself known through Jesus Christ, but as no. 4 indicates, the completion of Jesus's revelation takes place in the paschal mystery and in the 'final sending of the Spirit of truth.'

The New Direction of Barthian Theology

That the Second Vatican Council moved in this direction is not just an accident. The way toward the new model of revelation as God's self-disclosure had been thoroughly prepared, not least by the movement of neo-Orthodoxy within Protestant theology and the impulses given to a renewal of trinitarian theology by the pioneering work of Karl Barth.

Certainly to appreciate the meaning and the purpose of Barth's theology it is necessary to understand it historically. Barth was writing out of the context of the theology of the nineteenth century which was developed under the impact of the Enlightenment. It is significant that Kant, one of the greatest thinkers of the Enlightenment, rejected the Christian doctrine of the Trinity as a piece of useless speculation. He wrote:

> From the doctrine of the Trinity, taken literally, nothing what-soever can be gained for practical purposes, even if one believed that one comprehended it – and still less if one is conscious that it surpasses all our concepts.[2]

Under the impact of this type of thinking, Schleiermacher centred his theology in human experience, especially the religious feeling of total dependence on another. In his great work *The Christian Faith* Schleiermacher relegated the doctrine of the Trinity to an appendix. It is no accident that Barth means to turn Schleiermacher's theology on its head. In Barth's *Church Dogmatics* the Trinity is presented as the prolegomenon to all Christian theology. According to Barth, the doctrine of the Trinity provides the structure without which faith becomes unintelligible.

The entirety of Barth's theology is meant to be a response to Schleiermacher. Barth rejects the tradition of Enlightenment thinking which puts humankind at the centre of the universe. Barth wants to replace this anthropocentrism with a christocentrism. At the same time, for all Barth's insistence that theology has only one object, the Word of God, it is also clear that he has one eye constantly focused on the contemporary human situation. The man or woman of today lives in a world in which God seems to be distant, absent, silent or even dead. Barth's doctrine of revelation is meant to be a joyful response to the contemporary person who finds himself in this situation of darkness and anguish.

This background explains some of the cardinal points of Barth's doctrine of revelation. On the one hand, Barth insists that God in his own being is essentially hidden, concealed or veiled. Barth never tires of reiterating the fact of the transcendence of God. God is so far above us that there is no possibility of our ever reaching him. This is true first of all because we are creatures. God is in his heaven and we are on earth. This is all the more true because of the sinfulness of the human situation. According to the Bible, our sinfulness has cut us off from God. We have turned from him and ruptured our relationship. Friendship can only be restored from God's side. Given the unbridgeable chasm between God and humanity, Christian theology must radically reject anthropocentrism. Theology should not begin with the human subject or with religious experience, for it is never possible to ascend from this starting point to reach the living God.

At the same time Barth's theology is not negative, for the whole point of Barth's method is to lead to the recognition that what is impossible from below is possible from above; what is impossible anthropologically is possible christologically, and this is exactly the point of revelation.

For Barth, Christian faith is rooted in the fact that God has spoken. In uttering his Word into our human situation of darkness, God has given proof of his existence, he has given himself to be known as he is and he has established a relationship with us which we cannot establish ourselves. According to Barth, it is important to acknowledge the atheistic situation in which we live but one should not take the atheist too seriously, for the Christian has an unshakeable rock upon which to stand, namely the fact that God has spoken and his Word has penetrated into the silence which threatens us.

The first thing to say then about Barth's doctrine of revelation is that revelation is identified with the Word of God. In the *Church Dogmatics* Barth speaks of a three-fold sense of the Word of God. In its original and primary sense the Word of God is identified with Jesus Christ. There is an indissoluble unity and identity between God and his Word. Jesus Christ *is* God's Word. There are also two derivative senses of the Word, the Word of God in the Bible and the Word of God in the preaching and proclamation of the church. Jesus Christ can and does use these means, so that he can be found in them. For example, Jesus Christ can reveal himself to a believer who reads the scripture or hears a sermon, but there is not the same indissoluble link between God and his Word here as there is in the incarnate Jesus Christ.

Revelation then for Barth, in the primordial sense, is to be identified with Jesus Christ. His is a christological understanding of revelation. Something happens in Jesus Christ which has never happened before and which does not happen anywhere else. The hidden and transcendent God becomes unveiled and historical. Barth writes:

> The Christian apprehension of revelation is the response of man to the Word of God whose name is Jesus Christ. It is the Word of God who creates the Christian apprehension of revelation. From him it gains its content, its form and its limit.[3]

Barth stresses that this revelation is radically new: 'In Jesus Christ and in him alone, there enters upon the stage of human life that which is really *new*, and that which is hitherto unknown, because veiled and hidden.'[4] Revelation for Barth is also unique and unrepeatable. Since God has really communicated himself, there is nothing more for him to say. Jesus Christ is the eschatological event. It also follows for Barth that there are no other revelations. Only in this event is God to be found as he is. Barth does not hesitate to say that revelation is without analogy: '. . . revelation . . . has no analogies and is nowhere repeated. It stands alone and it speaks for itself. It receives light from nowhere else; the source of its light is in itself and in itself alone.'[5]

In the *Church Dogmatics* Barth also introduces an interpretative category to shed light on the nature of revelation. This is the category of the Lordship of God, a concept critical for Barth's trinitarian understanding of revelation. According to Barth, the word 'God' and the word 'Lord' are synonymous in the Bible. What the Bible reveals is the sovereignty of God. This is the constant theme of the Old Testament. In giving the ten commandments to the Israelites, God prefaces them with the fundamental truth of his sovereignty, 'I am the Lord your God, who brought you out of the land of Egypt, out of the house of bondage. You shall have no other gods before me.' (Ex. 20:2–3). This is also the message of the prophets, as we read for example in Isaiah, 'Turn to me and be saved, all the ends of the earth! For I am God and there is no other.' (Is. 45:22). Barth therefore chooses to construct his entire theology upon what he considers to be the fundamental testimony of the biblical witness: 'God reveals himself as Lord.'[6]

Barth claims that when one reflects upon the biblical testimony one sees that God's revelation of his Lordship occurs in a three-fold repetition. In fact this triple reiteration of his Lordship corresponds to the nature of revelation. What we see in the fact of revelation is that there is a three-fold distinction between God and the Revealer, God the Revelation, and the revealedness or impartation of this revelation.

First, there is God the Revealer. Through the act of revelation we discover who God is. God is the subject of his revelation. He is irreducibly subject and can never be made into an object to be manipulated. As acting subject, God is the Lord in his revelation. Without the act of revelation God would be essentially hidden. But in this sovereign act of his freedom God chooses to unveil himself. He puts himself in a relation to men and women. God the Revealer is also the source of his revelation. He is the abyss, the ground, the unfathomable mystery of the Godhead. In a certain sense Barth admits that the word God applies most originally and primordially to this source of the Godhead. Although the Revelation is identical with the Revealer, it is critical to observe the proper order of relationships. The revelation is derived from the unfathomable mystery which is the source of the Godhead.

If the first question in regard to revelation is: 'Who is God?', the second is: 'What does God do?' Here the answer is that God unveils himself and makes himself known. God communicates himself in such a way that he is identical with that which he reveals. Hence God does not reveal something about himself but himself as such. In fact God identifies himself with an historical event, with the person of Jesus of Nazareth. Jesus Christ is God's self-revelation in the primordial sense. Barth finds many diverse ways to illumine this truth. For example, he says that Jesus is God's self-interpretation, an interpretation which is so exact that God corresponds to himself in this event. He also says that God reiterates himself to the world in this event, that his eternity becomes temporal in this event. On the basis of the event of revelation, it is necessary both to make distinctions within God and to preserve the unity of Revealer and Revelation. In Barthian language, God differentiates himself from himself to become unlike himself and yet to remain himself.

The identity between God and his revelation allows God to remain irreducibly subject in the act of revelation. God does not create a *tertium quid* as an intermediary between himself and the world. In this case the humanity of Jesus would be understood in a reified way as something which God uses to express himself. Jesus's humanity is not something which God uses, but is rather God's self-expression. According to Barth, it was basically the mistake of Arius to overlook this point, thus making the Logos a medium between God and the world.

Having reflected on who God is and what God does in his revelation, we must proceed to a third question: 'What does God effect in his revelation?' Barth's answer is that God effects in us, the recipients of his revelation, communion with himself. The third mode of God's being in his revelation is what is meant by the Holy Spirit. It is necessary to complete the act of revelation with this third mode of God's being, otherwise revelation remains purely an event of the past. But that the revelation becomes contemporary, that it takes place in me, is the work of the Holy Spirit. And since it is only God who can effect communion with himself, this third mode of being must be as divine as the other two. Hence an analysis of God in his revelation reveals that God is and wants to be God in the three-fold repetition of Revealer, Revelation and Revealedness, i.e. as Father, Word and Holy Spirit. In other words, revelation implies a trinitarian interpretation of God.

Barth admits that the third distinction in God is the most nebulous and the hardest to grasp. It is easier to see the identity-in-difference of God the Revealer and his act of revelation. But for Barth an important point to remember is that God is always irreducibly subject in his revelation. This is important when the revelation event becomes contemporaneous in me. Without this third distinction, God would remain an object over against me. But Christian faith wants to say more than this. I do not just confront Christ as an object. Christ actually dwells in me, so that I know him as subject, as thou. This implies the third reiteration of God as subject, God the Holy Spirit.

It is interesting to note how agnostic Barth's trinitarian theology is. He tries to be thoroughly consistent in developing his doctrine of God strictly on the basis of revelation. As Barth sees it, revelation requires the believer to make distinctions in God. Without such distinctions we cannot give an adequate account of our experience of God on the basis of his Word. But it is part of the mystery of God that we cannot fathom the 'how' of God's triunity. To some extent we can see that the revelation is derived from the revealer and thus we get some insight into the creed's confession of the distinction between the unbegotten and the begotten. But Barth admits that it is far more difficult to get some insight into the third term of the revelation event. Classical theology spoke of procession and spiration. In general, Barth is sceptical of the Augustinian-Thomistic attempts to illumine the processions in terms of human analogies, such as that of intellect and will. All attempts along these lines are too anthropological for Barth and run the risk of human hubris. No, Barth believes that we must be content to leave the how of God's triunity shrouded in mystery. We must content ourselves to say only what needs to be said on the christological basis of God's revelation in Jesus. As Barth writes:

> We cannot establish the how of the divine processions and therefore of the divine modes of being. We cannot define the Father, the Son, and the Holy Ghost, i.e. we cannot delimit them the one from the other. We can only state that in revelation three who delimit themselves from one another are present, and if in our thinking we are not to go beyond revelation we must accept the fact that these three who delimit themselves from one another are antecedently a reality in God himself. We can state the fact of the divine processions and modes of being. But all our attempts to state the how of this delimitation will prove to be impossible.[7]

God's Real Relation to the World

We saw in Chapter I that the very analysis of the idea of creation implies a one-way relationship to God. On the other hand we noted that what is religiously important for the believer is the knowledge that God does want to relate himself to the world. But this is precisely the miracle of God's revelation. The German Jesuit theologian Peter Knauer, who has appropriated the Barthian tradition of the Word of God by way of the language theology of Gerhard Ebeling, affirms that the message of Christianity consists precisely in God's real involvement with the world through his Word, a Word which offers us communion with Himself. In speaking of revelation as a Word-event, Knauer writes:

> This being addressed by God in a human word is itself the event of community with God. Therefore the concept 'Word of God' in

its genuine sense is so to be understood, that it comprehends the entirety of God's saving act and concerns the entire reality of man. Therefore it is not to be completed through any further divine action, but it itself accomplishes what it says. In fact, salvation consists in being spoken to (Heb. 2:3). Therefore the 'Word of God' is not speech *about* the love of God to man, but it is itself the completion of this love, i.e. a Word-event.[8]

In a profound analysis of the concept of a Word-event Knauer argues that the real relation of God to the world implied in his addressing us can only be justified on the basis of a trinitarian understanding of God. Hence Knauer, like Barth, is arguing that the triune God is the necessary condition of possibility for God's revealing himself. His thesis is this: 'Man's being addressed by God can be understood as the real relation of God to the world, only if this presupposes an eternal relation of God to God, of the Father to the Son.'[9] For Knauer, the meaning of revelation is that the believer, the one addressed by God, knows himself loved with that very love which the Father has for the Son from all eternity. The measure or the standard of God's love for the world is not the world but the eternal Son. Thus in God's relating himself to the world, the world is not the terminus by which God's love is measured. The measure is the eternal love of Father and Son. Hence the constitutive term of God's love for the world is the inner-divine terminus of the divine Son into which the world is drawn. Hence Knauer writes, 'Only the trinitarian understanding of God makes it possible to unite the thesis of a self-communication of God to his creatures with the acknowledgement of his pure transcendence, absoluteness and uniqueness.'[10]

Knauer proceeds then to analyze the notion of God's self-communication against the background of the problem of the real relation of God to the world. The notion of the divine self-communication, Knauer maintains, can only be understood on the presupposition of the incarnation and the bestowal of the Spirit.

The Father shares his eternal love for the Son with the world by means of the incarnation. By means of his incarnate Word, God really relates himself to the world and says everything that he wants to say to us. One must be careful, however, to analyze the notion of the incarnation correctly. The humanity of Jesus is no independent reality on its own, a reality used by the Word. Such a conception would make a worldly, created reality the measure and the standard of God's love. This would be a mythological conception according to which the divine would be mixed with the worldly, so that God would become a part of a finite system. Also according to this conception the humanity would be divinized in a monophysitic way so that one could try to prove the divinity on the basis of the super-human and super-ordinary qualities of this humanity. According to the Council of Chalcedon, however, the divinity and the humanity of Jesus remain without separation but also without mixture. Therefore the humanity of Jesus remains strictly a humanity, like us in *all* things except sin. We cannot prove the divinity of Jesus on the basis of a super-ordinary humanity. According to Knauer, the divinity of Jesus can only be believed on the basis of the Word.

At the same time Knauer appeals to the classical notion of anhypostasis to explain that the terminus of God's love is not the creature but the divine Logos or Son. The doctrine of the anhypostasis refers to the problem of how we are to understand the relation of the divinity and the humanity in Jesus. In other words, how are we to understand the unity of the God-man? The Chalcedonian definition ruled out all dualistic Nestorian explanations. Jesus is not the addition of God and man. God does not take an already existing humanity to himself. Rather in God's expressing himself, in his becoming incarnate, the humanity comes to be as God's own humanity. The human nature, as created, from the first moment of its being, was always the humanity of the Logos. Pope Leo I expressed this truth in the phrase, *assumptione creatur*, i.e. in the act of being created the humanity was assumed by the Logos. The created humanity of Jesus was never a humanity on its own, was never an independent hypostasis, but was always the humanity of the one hypostasis of the divine Logos. Hence the term anhypostasis; 'an' comes from the Greek alpha-privative, a way of negating a phrase. Jesus's humanity is an-hypostatic, i.e. it is not an hypostasis on its own but is the humanity of the divine Logos. Knauer uses this model to explain how God can really relate himself to the world in the incarnation. The terminus of God's love according to this model is not the humanity but the Logos. Thus the measure of God's love is not a created reality but the eternal love of

Father and Son. The human nature is not the constitutive term of God's relation to the world. The constitutive term is the inner-trinitarian divine Logos. The basis of God's relation to the world is God's relation to himself.

However, all this is only of significance if we are indeed related to God, i.e. if we are caught up into this love of the Father and Son. This is what happens in faith. Faith is not just an intellectual act of assent. Faith is an existential relationship to God on the basis of God's offer of himself, an offer which accomplishes what it proposes. God so speaks to me that I enter into a relationship with the God who addresses me. Faith in this sense is only possible by the gift of God himself. In theological terms, this means that faith is the work of the Holy Spirit. The work of the incarnation remains incomplete until human beings are drawn into the love relationship of Father and Son, until the human person knows himself loved with the divine measure of the eternal love of Father for Son. This takes place when the Holy Spirit enables me to believe. In the act of faith divine revelation reaches its completion. The Father relates himself to the world and the human person is drawn into a real relation with God. But, as we now see, it is only the trinitarian foundation of revelation that renders these assertions intelligible.

God as Giver, Gift and Ground of Acceptance of the Gift

To complete this reflection on the relation between revelation and Trinity, it would be useful also to look at the theology of Karl Rahner, for among Catholic theologians he initiated a whole new chapter in trinitarian theology, by directing attention away from a speculative reflection upon the inner life of the Trinity toward the foundation of trinitarian faith in salvation history. As his ground-breaking article in *Mysterium Salutis* indicated, for him the Trinity is 'the transcendent origin of salvation history.'

In his *Foundations of Christian Faith*, Rahner notes that the term revelation must be understood to embrace three distinct but related experiences. First, there is natural revelation. This is God's disclosure of himself to every man or woman simply in virtue of his or her humanity. Perhaps the key term in Rahner's philosophical anthropology is transcendence. This term indicates that the human being is a dynamic propulsion beyond himself toward the Infinite. Like St Thomas Aquinas, Rahner understands the human subject according to the two faculties of intellect and will. In every act of knowing I am aware of some finite reality. But this finite reality in turn raises new questions for me. Hence knowledge is a dynamic process, a process in principle without a terminus. For Rahner this implies that knowledge is essentially ordered to Infinite Mystery. Rahner prefers to speak of Mystery, for this term indicates that the horizon of my knowledge is necessarily indefinable and ineffable. If I could define the Mystery, it would not be Mystery but rather some finite object.

At the same time, the human person is not only a knower. He is also a subject of freedom and love. But here as well his nature as transcendence reveals itself. In every act of choice, I am propelled beyond the finite object toward the Infinite. Every choice reveals a gap between the infinite yearning and longing of my heart and the finite realities with which I try to satisfy my desire. Hence also in every finite choice I also know implicitly the distant goal of my striving.

The conclusion is that in every human act God or the Holy Mystery is implicitly revealed as the term of transcendence. There is, therefore, a religious dimension to all human experience but this religious dimension is hidden, anonymous, nameless. In principle I cannot name the Mystery, for the Mystery is never an object in the world of my categorical experiences. Nevertheless in spite of its ineffable character, the Mystery is in fact more real than the objects of my everyday world. Because this Mystery is inescapably present in all my experiences, we can say that there is a natural revelation of God to every human person. As Rahner puts it:

> If God creates something other than himself and thereby creates it as something finite, if God creates spirit which recognizes the other as finite through its transcendence and hence in view of its ground, and if therefore at the same time it differentiates this ground as qualitatively and wholly other from what is merely finite, and as the ineffably and holy Mystery, this already implies a certain disclosure of God as the Infinite Mystery.[11]

Such a disclosure of God, however, hardly eliminates all the problems for the questioner. The type of revelation which the person experiences in natural revelation is of its nature problematical, for as Rahner shows, this God recedes every time we try to grasp him. Rahner refers to the Mystery as the 'asymptotic term' of transcendence[12] and in another place he writes, 'This . . . presents itself to us in the mode of withdrawal, of silence, of distance, of being always inexpressible, so that speaking of it, if it is to make sense, always requires listening to its silence.'[13] By its very nature, therefore, the natural revelation raises the further question whether God wishes to remain distant and silent or whether he wants to draw near and speak.

The believer is, of course, convinced that God has spoken and has drawn near to us through his revelation in Christ. Hence we come to the history of salvation properly so-called, God's strictly supernatural revelation, the offer not only of a share in existence through creation but the offer of his own divine being. As Rahner tirelessly repeats, God does not want to offer something other than himself but himself. The Giver and the Gift are identical in the act of revelation.

In order to understand this supernatural revelation, we must probe both the meaning of the incarnation and the supernatural elevation of the creature through grace. Let us begin with the reality of the incarnation.

In all of Rahner's theological writings on the incarnation, he is preoccupied with at least two problems. First of all, how can one present the church's faith in the incarnation in such a way that it does not appear to the man or woman of today as mythological and therefore unbelievable? Talk about God descending from heaven in the form of a man often seems to the contemporary person as a story of a pre-scientific age which is no longer credible. This is also linked to the problem that the simple believer often presents his faith in a monophysitic way, that is, Jesus is presented as God dressed up as a man. The humanity of Jesus is not understood as an autonomous humanity but rather as something used by the divinity. Thus, what is stressed is the divine nature. Jesus is seen as God's miraculous intervention in our human affairs, discontinuous with the rest of us, for example, by his power to work miracles, his omniscience, and his direct vision of God and the divine essence.

As early as Volume I of the *Theological Investigations*, Rahner perceived that at the heart of this problem is the conundrum of how we are to understand the unity of Christ, or in the language of

Chalcedon, the unity of the divine and human natures of Christ. Rahner also sees that this problem is not unique to christology. It also underlies the problem of the doctrine of creation and God's relation to the world. God and the world are not 'other' in the way that two categorical objects are distinct. If this were the case, God would not be God but God and the world would exist within a greater, all-embracing system. On the other hand, we must make a distinction between God and the world, otherwise we fall into pantheism. Rahner argues that the diversity between God and the world must be understood within a more profound unity, that is, God in the act of creation, both creates the diversity from himself and bridges the diversity by his creative power. As Rahner writes:

> The difference between God and the world is of such a nature that God establishes and is the difference of the world from himself, and for this reason he establishes the closest unity precisely in the differentiation.[14]

The same problem underlies the understanding of the incarnation. The definition of Chalcedon, according to which Jesus is one divine person in two natures, rules out two extreme interpretations of the unity of Jesus. One is Nestorian, according to which Jesus is a composite of the two natures. The other is monophysitic. According to this interpretation, after the incarnation there is only one nature, the divine nature in human flesh. Obviously such an interpretation does not do justice to his humanity and is implicitly docetic. The problem for Rahner, therefore, is how one can understand the unity of Jesus in such a way that room is left for a full autonomous humanity.

In Volume I of the *Theological Investigations*, Rahner reflects on this problem and proposes that the only solution is that the unity must be the ground of the diversity. In one and the same act, the Logos must create the humanity as a distinct, autonomous humanity but as a humanity in unity with the Logos as its humanity. That which makes the humanity *ek-sistent* as something diverse from God, and that which unites the nature with the Logos are strictly the same. Rahner writes:

> The only way in which Christ's *concrete* humanity may be con-

ceived of in itself as diverse from the Logos is by thinking of it *insofar as* it is united to the Logos. The unity with the Logos must constitute it in its diversity from him, that is, precisely as a human nature; the unity itself must be the ground of the diversity.[15]

In this way Rahner opens the way to a new approach to christology in which Jesus is understood as symbol, sacrament, or self-revelation of God; that is to say, Jesus is that finite human reality who is both diverse from God but is also at the same time so identical with God that he is God's perfect self-expression. As Rahner puts it, when God wants to express himself to the world what comes to be is Jesus of Nazareth. Or in alternate terminology, Jesus is the exteriorization of God or his *ek-stasis*. God does not give something different from himself but God gives his very self. As Rahner never ceases to affirm, the Giver and the Gift are identical. In Jesus, therefore, we have a humanity which precisely in its humanity is the disclosure of the divinity. There is the closest possible unity within differentiation between the humanity and the divinity. As Rahner puts it:

> We must learn to see that what is human in Jesus is not something human (and as such uninteresting for us in the world) and 'in addition' God as well (and in this respect alone important, this special character however always merely hovering above the human and forming its exterior setting, as it were). On the contrary, in this view the everyday human reality of this life is God's Ex-sistence in the sense cautiously determined above: it is human reality *and so* God's and *vice versa*.[16]

In a later essay Rahner uses the language of symbol to express this christology. God is the symbolized. Jesus is the symbol of God, but symbol understood not in the superficial sense of one being which refers to another absent reality, but in the profound metaphysical sense of one being which expresses itself through another being, which although diverse from it, is at the same time constitutive of its essence. At the end of his essay on the theology of symbol, Rahner notes that Jesus:

> . . . is the absolute symbol of God in the world, filled as nothing

else can be with what is symbolized. He is not merely the presence and revelation of what God is in himself. He is also the expressive presence of what – or rather, who – God wished to be, in free grace, to the world, in such a way, that this divine attitude once expressed, can never be reversed but is and remains final and unsurpassable.[17]

Does Rahner's symbol christology evacuate the traditional faith of the church of its meaning? When Rahner suggests the formula, 'Jesus is the symbol of God', is this a watering down of the Christian's belief in the incarnation? Are we still allowed to say, for example, that Jesus is God? From the previous explanation, I hope it is clear that Rahner is intending to offer us a contemporary interpretation of Chalcedon, not a refutation of it. He believes that his symbol christology says the same thing as the Chalcedonian formulation. In a provocative reflection upon this problem in *Foundations of Christian Faith*, Rahner argues that we may continue to say 'Jesus is God' if we understand the formula correctly, but he warns that the average believer is likely to interpret the formula in a monophysitic way. For example, in an ordinary proposition such as 'Peter is a man' the statement presupposes and expresses a real identity between the subject and the predicate. However, one cannot make such a real identification in the christological statement 'Jesus is God' without further ado, because according to Chalcedon the two natures exist not only unseparated (*adiairetos*) but also unmixed (*asynchytos*). As Rahner explains, 'In and according to the humanity which we see when we say "Jesus", Jesus "is" not God, and in and according to his divinity God "is" not man in the sense of a real identification.'[18] Thus there is always the danger in these 'is' formulas that the true meaning of Chalcedon is distorted and that one is understanding the formula in a monophysitic sense, i.e. the humanity is being mixed with the divinity in such a way that one is really taking the humanity as a mere mask or livery of the divinity. In fact the incarnation expresses a unique, deeply mysterious unity between realities which are really different and which are at an infinite distance from each other. This unity can only be perceived through an act of faith.

Rahner's christology, like Barth's, is based on the fact that God has really disclosed himself. In the incarnation there is a real identity between the Revealer and the Revelation, between the Giver and the Gift. This act of revelation takes place in our history. This is especially important for Rahner, because according to his anthropology, the human being is radically historical and hence any claim of salvation which by-passes his historicity can never fully redeem him, for it would fail to touch him where he lives in the world of space and time. At the same time Rahner sees that the categorical offer of salvation in itself is also insufficient to redeem the human person. A human being can only be fully redeemed if the offer of salvation touches him or her in the very depths of human subjectivity. This happens according to Rahner through God's offer of grace. Hence God's dealings with humanity are always bipolar. God works both transcendentally in the subject and categorically in history. In terms of the economy of salvation, this means that God works christologically and pneumatologically. Having already explained Rahner's understanding of Jesus Christ, I can now turn to his understanding of the working of the Holy Spirit in the depths of the subjectivity of every human person.

Of contemporary theologians, Rahner is certainly one of the greatest champions of God's offer of grace. In *Foundations of Christian Faith*, Rahner entitles his fourth chapter 'Man as the Event of God's Free and Forgiving Self-Communication'. This is very important, for it indicates how intimate is the relationship between grace and human subjectivity. Just as in his christology, so here too Rahner stresses that the Giver and the Gift are identical. Thus God so bestows himself on the creature that through grace he becomes an intrinsic, co-constitutive principle of the human subject himself.

A number of points for reflection are called for here. If the thesis above is correct, it implies, as Rahner realizes, that the primary understanding of grace must be that of uncreated grace. This is a departure from the scholastic tradition. For Rahner grace means the uncreated gift of God's own life.

Secondly, in order to illuminate the mystery of God's self-bestowal, Rahner appeals to the distinction between formal and efficient causality. In efficient causality, God creates an effect different from himself, such as in the act of creation. But in the gift of grace, he becomes a co-constitutive element of the human subject. This could be understood by analogy with formal causality in which a particular existent, a principle of being, is a constitutive element in another being by the fact that it communicates itself to this being. However, the category of formal causality could be misleading in that it could seem to imply a reduction of God's transcendence. Normally, when one speaks of formal causality in the Aristotelian sense, the formal and material causes are seen to be immanent within the being. The problem is how to understand God's bestowal of himself upon the creature without surrendering the divine transcendence or without making grace merely accidental or extrinsic to the creature. Rahner recognizes that he is using the term formal causality analogously (at times he speaks of semi-formal causality). In any case he wants to understand grace in such a way that the creature is elevated to participate in God's revelation of himself without ceasing to be a creature and God offers himself to become a constitutive element of the human subject's fulfilment without ceasing to be God. In an important passage in *Foundations of Christian Faith*, Rahner writes:

> God's self-communication is given not only as gift, but also as the necessary condition which makes possible an acceptance of the gift, which can allow the gift really to be God, and can prevent the gift in its acceptance from being changed from God into a finite and created gift which only represents God, but is not God himself. In order to be able to accept God without reducing him, as it were, in this acceptance to our finiteness, this acceptance must be borne by God himself. God's self-communication as offer is also the necessary condition which makes its acceptance possible. [19]

Naturally when Rahner is speaking about uncreated grace, he is speaking about the Holy Spirit. For he is not speaking about God in his self-expression in history. This is the Logos made flesh. But he is speaking about the other mode of God's self-communication, God the Holy Spirit, whose mission is to divinize the human subject and to render possible the acceptance of the gift of God's offer of himself.

However, at this point an important question arises: how are we to understand these two modes of God's self-communication to one another? The Christian tradition has always maintained that Christ is absolutely necessary for salvation. It has also maintained (consistently with that position) that all grace is the grace of Christ. On the other hand, Rahner is a strong advocate of the universality of grace. Grace is given to every person whatsoever, at least as an offer. If this is true, and if a person accepts this grace, of what additional significance is the incarnation?

There are two ways in which one could respond to these questions. First, Rahner appeals to another type of causality, final causality. All grace is the grace of Christ, for all grace is given in view of Christ. Christ was the intended goal of God's self-communication from all eternity. Christ was never merely an afterthought of God's purposes. Hence even the grace which is given temporally prior to the Christ-event is ontologically oriented to him. Secondly, all this makes sense ultimately if one plunges to the depths of God's trinitarian life. The bestowal of grace and the gift of the incarnation are two modes of God's self-communication. But they have an intrinsic relation to each other, for they are rooted in God's eternal being. The two modes of God's self-communication in time can only be held together in unity if they are a unity-in-differentiation in the divine life. This is, of course, Rahner's conviction of faith. God's movement out of himself into history through creation and through the work of the Holy Spirit are all ordered to Jesus Christ who is both God's perfect self-offer and simultaneously the perfect response to the offer. In turn, through the gift of grace each of us has the opportunity to participate in that self-communication of God and hence to be divinized. Grace and incarnation are complementary gifts.

In this section on Rahner's theology, I have spoken little in an explicit way of his trinitarian theology; the focus has been on incarnation and grace. In effect I have been concentrating on the presence of God in the history of salvation. But implicitly, all along, I have been talking about the Trinity. For if it is true that God really has communicated himself in our salvation history, i.e. if the one Holy Mystery has offered himself (and not something other than himself) in the incarnation and in grace, then it follows, as Rahner argues, that God in his own life must also exist in these three modes of being. If God has held nothing back in his revelation, then God in his own life is as he is in his revelation. If God in his revelation is three-fold, then God in his infinite Being is trinitarian Mystery.

There follows logically the thesis which has become commonplace since Rahner began writing on trinitarian theology, namely that the Trinity of the economy of salvation is the immanent Trinity and vice versa. However, as I hope is now clear, such a thesis is not, as Kant maintained, of no practical significance. It is far from just a speculative assertion. The affirmation of God's triunity is made in order to preserve and to make intelligible the experience we have of God in our salvation history. Ultimately this assertion of the triunity of God has the function of rendering intelligible the central conviction of faith, that the silent and distant Holy Mystery has drawn near to us in the radical proximity of our space and time and in the depths of our human subjectivity. As Rahner writes:

> It is only through this doctrine that we can take with radical seriousness and maintain without qualifications the simple statement which is at once so very incomprehensible and so very self-evident, namely that God himself as the abiding and Holy Mystery, as the incomprehensible ground of man's transcendent existence is not only the God of infinite distance, but also wants to be the God of absolute closeness in a true self-communication, and he is present in this way in the spiritual depths of our existence as well as in the concreteness of our corporeal history. Here lies the real meaning of the doctrine of the Trinity.[20]

The Economic and the Immanent Trinity

Before bringing this chapter to a close, it might be useful to say a few more words about the identity of the immanent and economic Trinity, for it is this insight toward which all our reflections in this chapter have been directed. First of all, it is worth noting that there is today a fairly wide consensus about this thesis in Catholic, Protestant and Orthodox theology. In addition to the development of this idea in Rahner, there is the witness of the Orthodox theologian J. Meyendorff who writes, 'God's Being for us belongs to his Being in himself.'[21] The same point is made by Barth when he writes, 'The reality of God in his revelation is not to be bracketed with an "only" as if somewhere behind the revelation there stood another reality of God; rather it is the case that the reality of God which encounters us in the revelation is his reality in all the depths of his eternity.'[22] Kasper expresses the same doctrine with a slightly different formula, 'Through Jesus Christ and in the Holy Spirit God is the salvation of man.'[23]

Kasper develops his position as follows.[24] First of all, human salvation can consist in nothing other than God himself. But God's salvation comes to us through Jesus Christ and in his Spirit. This salvation would be undermined if we did not really have to do with God himself. Thus God in the economy of salvation must correspond to God as he is in his own divine life.

Secondly, Kasper notes that the clearest instance of the identity between the immanent and the economic Trinity is the incarnation. Kasper accepts Rahner's argument that Jesus is the real symbol of God, i.e. that human reality in which the divine comes to perfect visible expression.

Finally, the salvation which Jesus brought us consists in our becoming through him sons and daughters of the Father. This self-communication of God becomes an event in us through the Holy Spirit whom the Son pours into our hearts. What Jesus has by nature, we have by grace. Hence God's indwelling in us has a trinitarian structure. God comes to us through his Son and in the Holy Spirit. Because there is a personal indwelling of the Spirit in us, we are united to the Son and through him go to the Father. If one removes this trinitarian structure of faith, one in effect undermines the entire experience of salvation.

At the same time, Kasper notes that the identity of the immanent and the economic Trinity is open to several false interpretations. One such would be to view the Trinity in salvation history as merely the temporal appearance of the eternal immanent Trinity. On the contrary, one must acknowledge that something new happens to God in the incarnation. By virtue of his becoming flesh, God has a new mode of being in the world. We witness this in the classical thesis that God became man. As Rahner insists, we cannot so water this down that nothing happens to God. In spite of the classical axiom of God's immutability, the incarnation implies that God really does 'become'. As Rahner puts it, even if God is unchangeable in himself, he does become in the other, i.e. in his humanity.[25] Rahner also warns us that it is insufficient to say merely that the change (i.e. the process of the human life and death of Jesus) took place in the created human nature of Jesus, for although this is true in itself, Rahner argues:

... if we say only this, we have overlooked and left unsaid the very thing which ultimately is the precise point of the whole assertion: that this very event we are talking about, this process of becoming, this time, this beginning and this fulfilment, is the event and the history of God himself.[26]

A second and perhaps more serious danger would be to dissolve the immanent Trinity in the economic Trinity of salvation history. This would be the doctrine that God can only be God, can only realize himself as divine by involving himself in history. This is the view of Hegel and also of American process philosophy and theology, and in some of his statements Moltmann comes close to affirming a similar position. But the immanent Trinity is not constituted by the economic Trinity. Rather, God freely decided to open himself to history. As Kasper puts it, 'in the thesis that the immanent Trinity is the economic Trinity, the sense of the word "is" is not that of an empty tautology, such as A=A. We are not talking about a static identity. Rather the "is" must be understood in the sense of an historical event. Perhaps it would be better to say that the immanent Trinity becomes the economic Trinity, for the "is" indicates a non-derivable, free, gracious historical presence of the immanent Trinity in the economy of salvation.'[27]

Conclusion

In this chapter I have tried to show that the specifically Christian understanding of God is rooted in the reality of God's revelation of himself. And we attempted to illuminate why an adequate hermeneutic of revelation leads to a trinitarian formulation of God's being. In the background was always the Kantian objection that the doctrine of the Trinity is an idle speculation divorced from human experience and beyond the limits of human comprehension. This is a misunderstanding rooted in a false approach to the Christian understanding of God which seeks to penetrate the mysteries of the divine life apart from the concrete events of our salvation history in which God gives himself to be known. On the other hand, our reflections in this chapter will also remain lifeless unless we move beyond a formal schematization of revelation and indicate the basis for this trinitarian scaffolding in the life of Jesus himself. It will be our task, therefore, in the following two chapters to probe the foundations for the Christian doctrine of God in Jesus's own awareness of his divine sonship and in his experience of the Spirit. We must then go on to ask how these pivotal experiences of Jesus were both tested and confirmed in the paschal mystery.

III

Jesus, the Son and Bearer of the Spirit

Introduction

The greatest danger that could arise on the basis of the previous chapter would be that one could regard the doctrine of the Trinity as merely a tautological corollary of the concept of revelation. This would make faith in the Trinity the kind of abstraction which the rationalism of the eighteenth and nineteenth century rightly wanted to avoid. Such is the charge which has been brought, for example, against Barth's trinitarian theology. In his magisterial work *God as the Mystery of the World*, Eberhard Jüngel points out that Barth can give the impression that the doctrine of the Trinity is a deduction from the proposition 'God reveals himself as Lord'. To overcome this impression, Jüngel argues that we must not only interpret the humanity of Jesus within the horizon of the faith in the triune God but even more importantly we must ground faith in the triune God in the context of the humanity of Jesus.[1] In effect this is also the suggestion of Robert Butterworth. Recognizing that contemporary approaches to dogmatics seek to ground doctrines in the actual Christian experience of God and in Christian praxis, he asserts, 'If the fundamental and distinctive experience of God, which underlies the development of the Christian doctrinal tradition in general and the doctrine of the Trinity in particular, is to be discovered anywhere, it is surely in Jesus's own human experience of God.'[2] He then goes on to suggest that Jesus's 'Abba experience', his consciousness of Sonship and possession of the Spirit are the seeds for the later doctrine of the Trinity. Let us then return to the New Testament witness and examine the biblical evidence for Jesus's unique experience of God which became the basis of Christians' experience of God as they learned to participate in Jesus's own vocation and destiny.

Jesus as the Son

There is no doubt that the New Testament attributes a unique identity to Jesus as God's only Son. This faith is attested primarily in the fourth gospel though Paul knows this theology as well. In Galatians, for example, he writes, 'God sent forth his Son, born of woman, born under the law, to redeem those who were under the law, so that we might receive adoption as sons.' (4:4–5). Nevertheless, it is the fourth evangelist who develops most fully the notion of Jesus's Sonship in the absolute sense. One could multiply the texts almost indefinitely but for our purposes here a few can suffice. There is, for example, in chapter three, the verse which recapitulates the entire Good News, 'God so loved the world that he gave his only Son, that whoever believes in him should not perish but have eternal life.' (3:16). Again in chapter five, it is to the Son in the absolute sense that God allots the role of judgement. 'The Father judges no one, but has given all judgement to the Son, that all may honour the Son, even as they honour the Father.' (5:22).

The difficulty, from the point of view of modern exegesis, is to know how much of this New Testament faith goes back to the historical Jesus himself. Certainly we know that in the Old Testament it was possible to attribute a special relationship of sonship *vis-à-vis* God to a human being without implying that this human being was divine. One thinks, for example, of the king who was considered to be exalted to divine sonship at the moment of his coronation. We witness this interpretation in the psalms, especially the well-known verse of Psalm 2:7: 'You are my Son, today I have begotten you.' This verse became an important source for messianic hopes and was applied to God's ideal king or messiah who was awaited by Israel. The problem then is how far the notion of divine sonship in the strict sense can be traced back to Jesus himself. Did Jesus claim to have a unique status as God's Son or is this a subsequent development of the post-resurrection church?

Here I accept the moderate view of such scholars as James Dunn, C. F. D. Moule, Martin Hengel and others that there is a significant development in the New Testament affirmations about Jesus but that this development does not imply a radical break or discontinuity with Jesus's self-understanding but is rather an unfolding after the resurrection of a claim that was implicitly present in Jesus from the beginning. In other words, I would not want to argue that Jesus explicitly claimed to be Son of God in the absolute sense which later trinitarian theology affirmed, i.e. the second person of the Trinity, ontologically equal to the Father, but I do believe that one can substantiate that the roots for this later doctrinal development can be found within Jesus's own unique experience of filiation in his special relation to God as Abba. Thus, for example, Hengel observes, 'Even if Jesus probably did not designate himself "Son of God" in so many words, the real root of the post-Easter title lies in the relationship to God as Father.'[3] The Cambridge exegete C. F. D. Moule adopts a similar position. He writes:

It is probably unrealistic to put notions of sonship into successive compartments, as though we could segregate a more or less humanistic, merely messianic use from a transcendental and theological use developing at a later stage. The indications are rather, that the words and practices of Jesus himself, together with the fact of the cross and its sequel, presented the friends of Jesus, from the earliest days, with a highly complex, multivalent set of associations already adhering to the single word 'Son'.[4]

There is virtually unanimous agreement today among exegetes that Jesus understood himself as the prophet of God's Kingdom. He proclaimed an imminent breaking-in of God's rule upon the world. He was sent by God to proclaim this proximate event as a joyful message for those willing to be converted and accept God's forgiveness. In the consciousness of Jesus, world history was in its eleventh hour. The moment of God's final and unsurpassable revelation was at hand. In Jesus's words and deeds, the kingly rule of God was already making itself felt. It would be but a short interval before the confirmation of this hidden beginning would be revealed for all to see. It is even more important to realize, however, the link which Jesus makes between himself, his teaching and his ministry. In his preaching and mission he affirms an indissoluble link between himself and the coming Kingdom. Acceptance or rejection of him will determine acceptance or rejection in the Kingdom when God's glory appears. All this amounts to an implicit christology during the life of Jesus, for Jesus assumes an intrinsic bond between God's salvation and himself. As I mentioned, this self-understanding at the basis of the mission of Jesus could be summed up in terms of eschatological prophecy. Reginald Fuller, the Anglican exegete, expresses it this way:

It is the unexpressed, implicit figure of the eschatological prophet which gives unity to all Jesus's historical activity, his proclamation, his teaching with exousia, his healings and exorcisms, his conduct in eating with the outcast and finally his death in the fulfilment of his prophetic mission. Take the implied self-understanding of his role in terms of the eschatological prophet away, and the whole ministry falls into a series of unrelated, if not meaningless fragments.[5]

But we might ask ourselves: where did Jesus derive this sense of mission, especially the authority with which he preached and acted, placing himself as he did above the law of Moses, calling upon no other authority except his own word ('Amen, amen, I say to you') and the authority of his God as his defence, so much so that he aroused the amazement of the people who declared that he does not teach like the scribes and the pharisees? To this question, the exegetes point precisely to Jesus's unique experience of Sonship. The English exegete Dunn writes, for example, 'Jesus's consciousness of sonship was probably a fundamental element in his self-consciousness out of which his other basic convictions about himself and his mission arose.'[6] The exegetical research of Schillebeeckx led him to draw the same conclusion in his book, *Jesus, An Experiment in Christology*:

> The source of this message and praxis, demolishing an oppressive notion of God, was his Abba experience, without which the picture of the historical Jesus is drastically marred, his message emasculated and his concrete praxis . . . is robbed of the meaning he himself gave to it.[7]

Let us look then a bit more closely at the New Testament evidence in regard to Jesus's experience of God as Father. The first thing which strikes us is the linguistic usage with which Jesus addresses God, namely the word 'Abba'. Although there are some 170 instances in the New Testament of Jesus addressing God as Father with the Greek word πατήρ and although undoubtedly many of these instances are the work of the theological redactor, it is virtually impossible to deny that the usage goes back to Jesus himself. One reason for this is that there is at least one instance in the gospels where the evangelist records the Aramaic word. In the story of Gethsemane in Mark 14:36 Jesus prays, 'Abba, Father, all things are possible to thee; remove this cup from me; yet not what I will but what thou wilt.' There are two other instances of the reminiscence of the word 'Abba' in the letters of St Paul. In Romans (8:15) Paul declares, 'For you did not receive the spirit of slavery to fall back into fear, but you have received the spirit of sonship. When we cry "Abba! Father!" it is the Spirit himself bearing witness with our spirit that we are children of God.' In another epistle, in Galatians (4:6), Paul writes, 'Because you are sons, God has sent the Spirit of his Son into our hearts, crying "Abba! Father!"' It is difficult to imagine how these instances of the Aramaic word could find their way into the New Testament if they are not preserving an authentic memory of the way Jesus spoke and prayed.

From the point of view of developing a theology of the life of Jesus, what is especially important here is that Jesus's way of praying marks a sharp departure from the tradition of the Old Testament. It is true that in the Old Testament God was considered to be the father of his people. There are numerous instances in which the title 'father' is used to express God's love for his people. In Exodus (4:22), we read, for example:

> The Lord said to Moses: 'You shall say to Pharoah, "Thus says the Lord, Israel is my first-born son, and I say to you, Let my son go that he may serve me; if you refuse to let him go, behold, I will slay your first-born."'

Again in Hosea, we come across the same idea in a verse which St Matthew later applies to Jesus in the infancy narratives, 'When Israel was a child, I loved him and out of Egypt I called my son.' (Hos. 11:1). The metaphor of fatherhood is used in the psalms to express God's mercy and compassion, 'As a father pities his children, so the Lord pities those who fear him.' (Ps. 103:13). However, what we note in these Old Testament texts is that the fatherhood of God is spoken of in the third person. It was not customary in the Old Testament to address God as father in prayer. Moreover, there is no instance of an individual addressing God as father in personal prayer. The fatherhood of God was seen more in terms of God's relation to the nation, to his people, Israel.

Moreover, it is not difficult to understand why there would be this reserve on the part of the Jewish people. The word 'Abba' was derived from secular usage. It was the child's word for its father and had the connotation of our English expression 'Daddy'. In other words it expressed familiarity and intimacy. By contrast the Jewish mentality stressed the sovereignty and transcendence of God. So great was the Jewish respect for God that the people refused to pronounce his name. That Jesus should dare to speak to God with such familiarity came as a shock. Here was a startling novelty. As Schillebeeckx observes:

> Of Jesus's standing out, in a historico-religious context, purely on the ground of his addressing God as Abba, there can be no question, *per se*. Jesus's uniqueness in his relationship to God undoubtedly lies in its unaffected simplicity; and the marks of that in late Judaism, though not absent, were really rare.[8]

Another feature is striking in the gospel portrayal of Jesus's prayer life. Jesus always prays to God as 'my Father'. And he always makes a distinction between 'my Father' and 'your Father'. In other words, Jesus always recognizes that he has a privileged relationship *vis-à-vis* his Abba. He does not put himself on the same level as his disciples. Rather he invites his disciples to share in his prayer experience when he teaches them the 'Our Father'. A study of this prayer also reveals a number of features which illuminate Jesus's self-understanding. For example, we indicated above that the centre of Jesus's mission was the coming of God's Kingdom and we suggested that the source of Jesus's sense of mission lay in his Abba-experience. But it is precisely the union of these two realities which we find in the Lord's prayer. Surely the central petition of this prayer is 'Thy Kingdom come'. But when we are told to pray this prayer and to beg for the coming of the Kingdom, we are also told to use that form of address which Jesus himself used. We are told to begin by addressing God as Father, as Abba. In other words we are being invited to share in Jesus's Sonship and to pray exactly as he prayed. A number of exegetes today have pointed out that the original context of the Lord's prayer was thoroughly eschatological, a fact which accords perfectly with the ministry of Jesus. In this eschatological prayer, the link between Jesus's Abba experience and the Kingdom reveals that sharing in God's fatherhood is part of the eschatological gift which Jesus offers us. In the nineteenth century, the fatherhood of God and the brotherhood of man were often seen to be the common property of the religious experience of humanity. But this is not the case. To be able to call God Abba is a gift one receives when one becomes a disciple of Jesus and is initiated into his unique experience of Sonship. This is why in the Christian tradition the Lord's prayer was always considered one of the unique treasures offered to the newly baptized, and in the eucharist it comes directly before the communion, in that part of the mass from which catechumens were excluded, as a sign that this is a prayer for fully initiated Christians. To be able to enter into an Abba relationship with God is part of the eschatological gift offered to us in Jesus.

Before leaving the question of Jesus's Sonship, I must say a word about the significant but controversial text which we find in Matthew (11:27). There Jesus says, 'All things have been delivered to me by my Father, and no one knows the Son except the Father, and no one knows the Father except the Son and anyone to whom the Son chooses to reveal him.' The text has been called the Johannine thunderbolt in the synoptic gospels. At first glance it seems a perfect instance of the type of absolute Sonship attributed to Jesus in the fourth gospel, the kind of christology which we have seen is a great development from the message of Jesus. For a long time exegetes considered this passage a theological reflection of the Christian community put on the lips of Jesus. However, the German scholar Joachim Jeremias has raised serious objections against this assumption. He has shown, for example, that there are no linguistic reasons for rejecting this logion as authentic. It is possible to work back from the Greek text to an Aramaic original which Jesus could have said. Jeremias admits that in its present form it reflects a post-resurrectional christology but he suggests that underlying the saying is a 'Son' christology which goes back to Jesus himself. Jeremias believes that at the base of the saying, there is a metaphor based on normal Jewish, Palestinian life. Just as a father has an intimate knowledge of his son, initiates him into his trade, and just as a good Jewish father introduces him to the Torah, so God has this kind of relationship with Jesus. The logion, then, does not in its origins speak of a christology of absolute Sonship in the trinitarian sense but it points to the absolute authority of Jesus based on his unique intimacy with the Father. Jesus is the bearer of a revelation which has not been communicated to any other person. His mission is unique and without parallel in the history of the world. Such an interpretation fits in with other sayings of Jesus in which he claims to be the bearer of God's definitive revelation and salvation. One thinks, for example, of the preceding verses in St Matthew's gospel, 'I praise thee, Father, Lord of heaven and earth, that thou didst hide these things from the wise and intelligent and didst reveal them to babes;' or of Mark (4:11) where Jesus declares, 'To you has been given the mystery of the Kingdom of God; but for those outside everything is in parables.' As Schillebeeckx says:

> In Jesus's time what the abba signified for his son was authority and instruction: the father is the authority and the teacher. Being a son meant 'belonging to'; and one demonstrated this sonship by carrying out father's instructions. Thus the son receives everything from the father ... The son also receives from the father 'missions', tasks which in the name of his father he has to make his own.[9]

This understanding of the Abba–Son relationship, which probably underlies Matthew (11:27), illumines Jesus's relation to his Abba as the source for his understanding of his mission and the sense of authority with which he carried it out.

A number of years ago, the American exegete, Raymond Brown, responding to the anxiety of those who fear that modern critical methods undermine the faith of the church, pointed out, somewhat humorously, that even if modern exegesis rejected many of the sayings of Jesus as authentic, at least no modern exegete would deny that there are two words which indisputably go back to Jesus himself. One of these words is 'Amen' and Jesus's unique use of it reveals the depth and extent of his perception of his authority. The other word is 'Abba', the testimony of his unique prayer experience. Brown reflects that even on the basis of these two words one could go a long way toward answering the gospel question: 'Who do men say that I am?' On the basis of Jesus's way of praying, I would not have any titles such as Son of God but I would know that:

> Jesus thinks he has the right to pray to God in the intimate, family language of the time; he addresses God as a little child

addresses his father, while nobody else does, and what is more, thinks he has the right to teach everybody else that they can pray to God that way, if they follow him.

Brown draws the conclusion: 'That would not tell me that Jesus is the Son of God, but it would tell me how the church came to understand that he was the Son of God.'[10]

Jesus as Bearer of the Spirit

When one looks at the New Testament record and compares it with the history of Christian doctrine one notices a remarkable discrepancy. Whereas a significant model for interpreting Jesus in the New Testament is that of one led by the Spirit, this model has a brief career in Christian dogmatics, probably because of the christological controversies of the fourth century. Faced with heterodox theologians who denied the eternal equality of Jesus with the Father, the church abandoned a Spirit-christology which could so easily seem to lead to a kind of adoptionism, i.e. the doctrine that Jesus is a mere man but with a unique endowment of the Holy Spirit.

Nonetheless the exegetical discoveries of this century have made us aware that there are diverse christologies in the New Testament, and for the biblical writers one significant way of interpreting Jesus was that of bearer of the Spirit. It is important for us to recover this perspective today because it helps us to understand both Jesus's relation to the Old Testament and his relation to us. As the Second Vatican Council pointed out, there is one and the same Spirit in Christ and in us. (*Lumen Gentium*, no. 7).

When we take even a superficial glance at the New Testament, we note first of all that there is no aspect of the life of Jesus which is not related to the Spirit in the minds of the New Testament writers. According to St Luke, Jesus is conceived when the Holy Spirit comes upon Mary and the power of the Most High overshadows her. (Lk. 1:35). In the baptism, the Spirit of God descends upon Jesus, thus inaugurating his public ministry and revealing for all to see that he is installed in the office of God's messiah (Mk. 1: 10–11). After his baptism, Jesus is led into the desert by the power of the Spirit. (Mk. 1:12). St Luke indicates that Jesus begins his public ministry by referring to Isaiah 61: 'The Spirit of the Lord is upon me, because he has anointed me to preach good news to the poor.'

(Lk. 4: 18). On the cross Jesus offers himself to the Father in the Holy Spirit (Heb. 9:14) and in the resurrection St Paul says that he became a life-giving Spirit (1 Cor. 15:45). In one of the kerygmatic speeches of Peter in Acts, the notion of Jesus's anointing with the Spirit is a central feature in the early Christian preaching about him, 'You know how God anointed Jesus of Nazareth with the Holy Spirit and with power; how he went about doing good and healing all that were oppressed by the devil, for God was with him.' (Acts 10: 38).

There is no doubt then that the New Testament interprets Jesus's identity and mission in terms of the category 'Spirit'. However, as in the case of Jesus's Sonship, the difficulty is to know how much this interpretation goes back to Jesus himself. Perhaps the best place to begin would be with Jesus's self-understanding as a prophet. We have already seen that implicit in Jesus's whole ministry is the figure of the eschatological prophet of the Kingdom. In the Old Testament the prophets received the Spirit of God to preach the Word of God in a unique situation. The prophet is a minister of God's word in the power of the Spirit. An interesting witness to this can be found in 2 Kings 2 where Elijah is taken up to heaven and passes on his spirit of prophecy to Elisha. Elisha's request before the departure of Elijah is simply this: 'I pray you, let me inherit a double share of your spirit.' (v. 9). Already in the bestowal of the spirit of prophecy upon the disciple Elisha, we see a foreshadowing of Jesus's gift of the Holy Spirit to his disciples.

There is also another important factor to notice, namely that after the exile, prophecy was considered to have died out in Israel. Nonetheless there was the hope that in the last days God would pour out his Spirit anew and prophets would live again in Israel. In the book of Joel there is a witness to this hope, a hope which Christians believed was fulfilled in the event of Pentecost. Joel's prophecy says: 'And in the last days it shall be, God declares, that I will pour out my Spirit upon all flesh, and your sons and your daughters shall prophesy, and your young men shall see visions and your old men shall dream dreams; yes, and on my manservants and my maidservants in those days I will pour out my Spirit; and they shall prophesy.' (Joel 2:28–29; Acts 2:17–18).

What we witness in the life of Jesus is precisely a fulfilment of these expectations. First of all, he preaches God's word in the unique situation of the last days. Not only does he preach this word but he incarnates it in saving deeds, for example, his healings and his table fellowship with tax-collectors and sinners. Moreover he performs just the kind of symbolic actions which the prophets of old had done. Hosea married a prostitute as a symbol of God's union with an adulterous people. Jeremiah remained celibate and without offspring as a sign of God's judgement on Israel. So too Jesus multiplies the loaves and the fishes as a sign of the eschatological feast of the Kingdom and of the reliving of the manna experience of the desert, he cleanses the temple as a sign of God's judgement on the worship of Israel, he curses the fig tree and causes it to wither as a sign of Israel's rejection, he enters Jerusalem seated on a donkey as a symbolic gesture of the nature of his reign.

In addition, it is clear that in his own lifetime Jesus was regarded as a prophet. In response to his question, 'Who do men say that I am?' (Mk. 8:27–28), the disciples reply, 'John the Baptist; and others say, Elijah; and others one of the prophets.' But not only do others regard Jesus as a prophet, he himself interprets his death in prophetic terms. In Luke 13, Jesus says:

> Nevertheless I must go on my way today and tomorrow and the day following; for it cannot be that a prophet should perish away from Jerusalem. O Jerusalem, Jerusalem, killing the prophets and stoning those who are sent to you. How often would I have gathered your children together as a hen gathers her brood under her wings and you would not. (vv. 33–34).

The conclusion is therefore that the category of prophecy is very suitable to interpret Jesus's self-understanding and mission, although as with all categories from the Old Testament, Jesus both fulfils them and shatters their limitations. Nevertheless as a prophet Jesus is precisely the one filled with the Spirit of God as none of his predecessors had been.

A second indication of Jesus's relation to the Spirit is his ministry of exorcism. Although there have been some rationalistic attempts to demythologize the miracles, there is a virtual unanimity as regards the fact that Jesus performed both healings and exorcisms. The exorcist activity is especially important, for it reveals an important dimension of Jesus's activity as prophet of the Kingdom of

God. God's rule is making itself felt in a situation of conflict. The coming of God's Kingdom is taking place with power. There is a universal, cosmic struggle between the power of God and the power of Satan. For a Jew, God is king by virtue of his work as creator, also in virtue of his covenant with Israel. But in a certain sense, God's kingship is still outstanding, for as long as there is sickness, death, injustice, oppression, God's Kingdom is not fully manifest. For a Jew there is no question of God's supreme Lordship and power over Satan. Nevertheless in the satanic struggles of the present age, one must place one's hope in God's eschatological victory over Satan. In Jesus's ministry and especially in his exorcist activity there is a cogent symbol that God's Lordship is making itself felt with power. The decisive victory is at hand. Jesus is the stronger one, with the power to break even Satan's might. From our point of view here, of critical importance is the logion in which Jesus links his ministry of exorcism with his prophetic announcement of the Kingdom. There are two redactions of this logion in the New Testament. The context is Jesus's casting out a demon from a man who is dumb. His critics bring the charge that he casts out demons by the power of Beelzebul. Jesus replies that Satan cannot be divided against himself and goes on to assert the link between this ministry of his and the irruption of God's Kingdom. According to Luke (11:20), Jesus says, 'But if it is by the finger of God that I cast out demons, then the Kingdom of God has come upon you.' According to Matthew (12:28), Jesus says, 'But if it is by the Spirit of God that I cast out devils, then the Kingdom of God has come upon you.' It is difficult to say which of these versions is original; but, in any case, it is not important, for the finger of God is a metaphorical way of speaking about God's power. What is important is that Jesus undoubtedly engaged in exorcist activity and that this activity was an important facet of his prophetic work of announcing the Kingdom of God and that this ministry was seen by the early church precisely as a sign that Jesus lived and worked from a unique possession of God's Spirit.

We come now to another important element in the New Testament interpretation of Jesus, the use of Isaiah 61. This poem, which recalls the servant songs of chapters 42 to 53, pictures the servant of the Lord as one especially endowed with the Spirit to bring God's message of salvation to the poor and oppressed. The servant declares, 'The Spirit of the Lord is upon me, because the Lord has anointed me to bring good tidings to the afflicted; he has sent me to bind up the broken-hearted, to proclaim liberty to the captives and the opening of the prison to those who are bound; to proclaim the year of the Lord's favour.' (vs. 1–2). One is immediately struck by the fact that the passage figures prominently in the gospel portrait of Jesus in the third gospel. In the inaugural scene of Jesus's ministry in Luke 4, the evangelist constructs the beginning of Jesus's ministry in the synagogue where Jesus took the book of the scriptures, opened it to this passage of Isaiah and proclaimed, 'Today this scripture has been fulfilled in your hearing.' Clearly for St Luke this inauguration of the ministry of Jesus is meant to provide the interpretative clue for understanding the life and mission of Jesus. He is that eschatological figure of salvation endowed with God's Spirit in the end-time, with the mission to proclaim the word of God's gracious and forgiving visitation of his people. Again, however, we encounter the difficulty whether we can take this text as an historical reminiscence of what Jesus actually did. Here the majority of the exegetes agree that the scene, as we have it in St Luke's gospel, is a theological construction. However, James Dunn argues that there is still good reason to believe that Isaiah 61 played an important part in Jesus's own consciousness, even if the scene in Luke 4 is a later redaction.[11]

The first reason for this is that a similar idea is at the heart of the beatitudes, which surely go back to Jesus himself. In the first beatitude Jesus declares, 'Blessed are you poor, for yours is the Kingdom of God.' (Lk. 6:20). Just as in Isaiah 61, here Jesus places the poor at the centre of his preaching and he declares them blessed precisely because they are the ones who are in a position of receptivity to hear the good news of the arrival of God's Kingdom. The other text in which there is a strong reminiscence of Isaiah 61 is that of Matthew 11:2–6 in which John the Baptist sends a delegation to Jesus to inquire if he really is the expected one of Israel. In the perspective of Jesus's ministry, the perplexity of John the Baptist is fully intelligible. The New Testament memories of John the Baptist portray him as a fiery prophet like Elijah in the Old Testament. His is a message of the impending judgement of God from which no one will be able to escape. St Matthew recalls his words, 'You brood of vipers! Who warned you to flee from the wrath to come?' John expects one to come after him but he is one who will baptize with fire like Elijah did in the Old Testament (Mt. 3:11). In this context we can see how

John the Baptist is puzzled by Jesus. Jesus did follow upon his ministry, only commencing his mission when John the Baptist was put into prison. But Jesus was not the type of figure John expected: he was a messenger of mercy, the Father's amnesty at the eleventh hour, and Jesus's conduct of eating with tax-collectors and sinners surely challenged John's assumptions of who God would send after him. Hence his delegation to Jesus. But Jesus's response to John is precisely in terms of Isaiah 61: 'Go and tell John what you hear and see: the blind receive their sight and the lame walk, lepers are cleansed and the deaf hear, and the dead are raised up, and the poor have the good news preached to them.' (Mt. 11:4–5). As Dunn remarks, the response to the question fits so perfectly with the situation of John's perplexity that there is no reason why we should not think that indeed this is how Jesus interpreted his mission.[12] He saw himself as fulfilling the role of the servant endowed with God's Spirit as foretold in Isaiah 61. Not only, therefore, did Jesus have a unique sense of his relationship to his God as Abba but he also knew himself as unique bearer of the Spirit. Thus Dunn concludes, 'Spirit and Sonship, Sonship and Spirit, are but two aspects of the one experience of God out of which Jesus lived and ministered.'[13]

The Experience of the Baptism

If there is any place in the New Testament where the Sonship of Jesus and his possession of the Spirit come into a close harmony it is in the story of the baptism. We are told that after the baptism, the heavens opened and the Spirit descended upon him and the Father spoke the words, 'Thou art my beloved Son; with thee I am well-pleased.' A number of observations immediately come to mind. First of all, the reference to the Son calls to mind the verse of Psalm 2:7, 'You are my Son, today I have begotten you.' This verse in the psalm refers to the anointing of the king. The king becomes God's Son by his royal anointing. But here Jesus's Sonship and his messianic office are linked together by means of the Spirit. As Heribert Mühlen notes, Old Testament messianology is being reinterpreted in a pneumatic way.[14] In the mind of the evangelist, the baptism is Jesus's installation in the office of messiah. This scene represents his anointing for his mission. From this moment he begins his task endowed with the power of the Spirit.

There is, however, another point of capital significance. The very same elements which we see linked together in the baptism of Jesus, namely baptism, Sonship and possession of the Spirit are the same three elements which are linked together in the theology of Christian baptism. In baptism we receive the new life of the Spirit which enables us to share in the inheritance of Jesus as participators in his Sonship. These are recurring themes in Pauline theology such as we find in Romans (8:10f., 15) and Galatians (4:6). However, there is also a remarkable transfiguration of the understanding of baptism. In the ancient world, water was almost universally used as a religious symbol but primarily in the sense of a cleansing or purification. However, in Pauline theology, the water of baptism has a more profound significance. Here it becomes a symbol of death and new life, in fact of resurrection through death. Water is not just cleansing but also evocative of destructive power. To go into the water of baptism is to drown, that is, to be swallowed up in the death of Jesus, so that one can be reborn with him to eternal life. This is the profound significance of Romans 6:3–4, 'Do you not know that all of us who have been baptized into Christ Jesus were baptized into his death? We were buried therefore with him by baptism into death, so that as Christ was raised from the dead by the glory of the Father, we too might walk in newness of life.' C. F. D. Moule asks how we can explain such a startling transformation. Is this merely the creative genius of the early church and the New Testament writers? Moule thinks that such an explanation is implausible.[15] Moreover, there are hints in the New Testament of such a reinterpretation of baptism which could develop into the later Christian theology. There is, for example, the memory of the dominical sayings in Mark (10:38) and Luke (12:50). In the first passage Jesus asks his disciples, 'Are you able to drink the cup that I drink or to be baptized with the baptism with which I am baptized?' In the second text, Jesus clearly refers to his own suffering and death when he says, 'I have a baptism to be baptized with and how I am constrained until it is accomplished!' Thus in the life of Jesus we see not only an association with baptism, Sonship and possession of the Spirit, but we have more than a hint that Jesus understood his vocation as Son and as bearer of the Spirit to involve a surrender of his life.

This idea can perhaps be further substantiated if we look at the trial scene in Mark 14. The climax of the trial in Mark's gospel no doubt occurs in the question of the high priest: 'Are you the Christ?'

The high priest thus directly puts the question as to Jesus's messianic identity. But we have already seen that, in the Old Testament, messianic kingship is linked to divine Sonship and that, in the New Testament, both are related to the possession of the Spirit. Here in the trial scene, we find that Jesus makes another remarkable association of symbols. He publicly proclaims his messianic identity for the first time in Mark's gospel and then goes on to say, 'You will see the Son of Man sitting at the right hand of Power, and coming with the clouds of heaven.' (v. 62). Here, therefore, Jesus is also identifying himself with the figure of the Old Testament Son of Man. Now of course the whole concept of the Son of Man is disputed but many exegetes would agree with Moule that the background of the saying is in Daniel 7:13. The problem is how to interpret the passage in Daniel and its relation to Jesus. Moule makes the following illuminating suggestion. In Daniel 7:13, the figure of the Son of Man is a human figure representing the persecuted, but loyal, people of Israel. This faithful servant will be vindicated on the last day and will be brought before the divine throne and the Ancient of Days. But the same figure is a perfect symbol to represent the person and mission of Jesus. According to Moule, 'Son of Man' is not a title applied to Jesus, but a symbol of his vocation to be utterly loyal, even to death, in the confidence of ultimate vindication in the heavenly court. The only difficulty is that in the Old Testament passage the figure of the Son of Man is taken to the heavenly court for vindication whereas here he is being manifested to the world in judgement. The *prima facie* difference between the two is, however, on deeper reflection, only an invitation to see the more profound unity of the two. In Moule's words, 'The glory of the human figure in heaven *is* his investiture as Judge of the earth.'[16] Hence Moule argues that 'Son of Man' is one of the most important symbols used by Jesus himself to describe his vocation.

The upshot of these exegetical reflections is that even in the life of Jesus himself there was a profound sense of his being Son in a unique sense *vis-à-vis* his Abba and of his being a unique bearer of the Spirit. If these experiences are linked to other dimensions of the New Testament portrait of Jesus such as his baptism, his use of baptismal language, his employment of the symbol Son of Man, one sees that Jesus's understanding of his Sonship and of his possession of the Spirit also had a unique orientation. Both had a profound link with the filial vocation of obedience toward his Father, an obedience which Jesus could see would lead him to the supreme surrender of his life on the cross. Thus Moule concludes that one of the clearest messages to emerge from the gospels is that it is the suffering Son of Man:

> . . . who is to be gloriously vindicated, that the meaning of greatness is service, that to be God's Son means to be dedicated unconditionally to God's purposes, even to death. It is therefore organic to the ministry of Jesus that the Son of God shows himself as the frail and vulnerable Son of Man. The two are identical in reality, long before ingenious exegetical connections are spun around them.[17]

According to Moule, therefore, there is a whole network of traditions about Jesus which led to a radical reinterpretation of what it meant to be Son of God. This process of reinterpretation undoubtedly went on after the death and resurrection of Jesus when the full implications of Jesus's Sonship began to dawn on the early Christian community. Creative this reinterpretation surely was but radically discontinuous with Jesus's own self-understanding it was not.

Conclusion

Our reflections in this chapter have sought to situate later church formulations of the Christian experience of God in the New Testament data and more particularly in the foundational experience of Jesus himself. We have seen that there is good reason to believe that Jesus thought of himself as Son of God and bearer of the Spirit. But we have also seen that he reinterpreted these ideas in terms of a unique vocation of obedience, an obedience which would lead him to the cross. At the centre of our Christian experience is the paschal mystery of Jesus, his passover from death to the glory of the Father. It is now most important for us to ask and to reflect upon how Jesus lived his experience of Sonship and of the Spirit in that supreme moment of crisis, the crucifixion, in which his Abba-experience was tested to the full and in which his experience of intimacy with his Father seemed to be shattered in the impenetrable darkness of God-forsakenness.

IV

Trinity and the Paschal Mystery

We have seen that the centre of Jesus's consciousness was his unique relationship to God as Abba. If we presuppose that 'person' is a concept which expresses a relation, we can go so far as to say that 'It is his relationship to the Father that constitutes the essence of his person.'[1] Out of this intimacy arose his sense of mission. Jesus claims to be the bearer of a unique revelation, 'All things have been given to me by my Father and no one knows the Father except the Son and anyone to whom the Son chooses to reveal him.' (Mt. 11:27). More concretely this revelation consisted in the fact of announcing and making present God's rule. In Jesus's preaching and ministry, God's final revelation of himself, including his victory over sin, death and other powers of destruction, was making itself felt. Hence what we see in the life of Jesus is God's becoming historical. God is drawing near to the world, so that history is opened to receive him as its true future.

However, if the relation of God to the world in revelation can only be grasped historically, the same is true of Jesus's relation to the Father. His rapport with his Father and his perception of his mission developed historically. Many exegetes thus distinguish between his early sense of mission in Galilee and his later perception after the crisis which led him to Jerusalem and the cross.

From the gospel reports, it seems that Jesus's early preaching and ministry met with a measure of success. And if we are not to think of Jesus as play-acting there is no reason not to believe that his urgent appeal to the people was a hope-filled summons to Israel on the part of Jesus. Jesus trusted that God's final redeeming act was very near and he summoned his people at the eleventh hour to prepare for the coming day of the Lord. But all the gospels report that after a certain interval there was a hardening of heart and a resistance to Jesus's work which provoked a great crisis in Jesus's life. A witness to this is the geographical fact that Jesus abandons the heart of Galilee and heads to Caesarea Philippi and then to the ten towns of the Decapolis. This break is situated in chapter eight of St Mark's gospel and in chapter thirteen of St Matthew's. Jesus stops talking to the crowds and concentrates on his own disciples who misunderstand the nature of his mission. There is also a witness to the same break in the fourth gospel. After the miracle of the loaves, the masses abandon him. (John 6:66). There is opposition to him and two attempts to stone him. (John 8:59; 10:31, 39). He is left only with the twelve disciples. As a result of this crisis, Jesus decides to go to Jerusalem and throw down the gauntlet of his challenge in the heart of the nation's capital. Dramatically St Luke reports: 'When the days drew near for him to be received up, he set his face to go to Jerusalem.' (9:51).

There are two aspects of this crisis which we could profitably reflect upon here. The first is Jesus's attitude toward his death. There is no doubt that the New Testament proclaims that Jesus's death did not catch him unawares. Jesus is not the victim of a tragic fate. In fact there are many passages which speak of Jesus freely offering his life as an expiatory sacrifice. Without any doubt, in the light of the resurrection, the church could look back upon the death of Jesus and see in it the self-offering of Jesus, a sacrifice by which we are reconciled to God. This faith is reflected in the accounts of the institution of the eucharist at the Last Supper where Jesus offers his body and blood 'for many'. The early Christian community saw in Jesus the figure of the suffering servant spoken of by Isaiah. The difficulty is to know how far this faith of the early church can be projected back into the explicit consciousness of Jesus himself. One thing, however, which we can say without any doubt is that Jesus foresaw and accepted his death as part of his fidelity to his heavenly Father and the mission which he had received from him. We have already seen, for example, that Jesus made a conscious decision to go to Jerusalem. He could have had very little doubt that with this decision he was reckoning with the possibility of death. He had already met with hostility and rejection. He had witnessed the fate of John the Baptist, and he interpreted his own life and destiny in terms of the prophets.

> Nevertheless I must go on my way today and tomorrow and the day following; for it cannot be that a prophet should perish away from Jerusalem. O Jerusalem, Jerusalem, killing the prophets and stoning those who are sent to you. How often would I have gathered your children together as a hen gathers her brood under her wings, but you would not! (Lk. 13:33–34).

Thus historically speaking, we can see that Jesus is caught between two loyalties which he refuses to surrender – he remains steadfast in loyalty to his mission, he represents God's mercy to sinful humanity to the end, and at the same time, he stands on the side of men and women, representing us before God to the end, and he lets himself be crushed by our rejection. The death of Jesus results from his refusal to compromise either loyalty.

The other aspect of this crisis is precisely the dimension of a crisis of faith. First of all, we must ask if Jesus lived by faith. In the Middle Ages, St Thomas answered this question negatively because he held that Jesus possessed the beatific vision at every moment of his life. Today, most theologians would hold that such a beatific vision is incompatible with Jesus's human knowledge and human freedom during his state of earthly pilgrimage. Many theologians would want to take seriously the kenosis of Jesus in the act of becoming incarnate and consequently they distinguish between two stages of Jesus's human history, the stage of pilgrimage and the stage of completion in the resurrection. If Jesus really became human, it would seem that he had to grow in knowledge. It would also seem that if he really accepted our condition, his freedom was conditioned by a certain ignorance. As Rahner points out, if Jesus always had a clear omniscience and beatifying presence of the Father, it is hard to see how any human choice was possible for him. This is not to say that Jesus was unclear about his identity or about his intimacy with the Father or about his mission from the Father, but only that all of these facets of his experience existed for him under the conditions of space and time.

In this sense Jesus is the supreme example of faith, faith being understood as the complete surrender to God under the conditions of human darkness and in the face of the threats which human life poses. In this way one could appropriate the theology of the Letter to the Hebrews and not see Jesus as dispensed from faith but rather as the model of faith, as the catalyst of faith, he who makes faith possible. The author of Hebrews writes, 'Let us look to Jesus, the pioneer and perfector of our faith, who for the joy that was set before him endured the cross, despising the shame, and is seated at the right hand of the throne of God.' (12:2).

In this perspective I would emphasize the trust dimension of faith. Jesus throughout his whole life surrenders himself into the hands of God, without trying to set the agenda, and without asking for guarantees he lets God be God. But precisely when we regard the faith of Jesus in this way, we can see two stages of his faith. The first stage consisted in the Galilean period. Jesus receives from the Father the revelation, the mission to preach the Kingdom. From the moment of the baptism, anointed for this mission, he proclaims in word and deed the impending rule of the Father. But in the moment of the Galilean crisis, his faith is tested. He is challenged to live on a deeper level of faith. As Sobrino has pointed out, we need not understand the crisis of faith as a crisis of doubt. The temptation against faith which Jesus experienced is grounded not in doubt but in the vicissitudes of life itself. In the Galilean crisis, Jesus finds himself progressively more alone. The masses walk away, the religious leaders harden their hearts. The disciples fail to understand. We see here a movement which leads directly to the cross where Jesus finds himself radically alone, apparently deserted even by the God he called Abba. According to Sobrino, Jesus overcomes the crisis of faith but this crisis has thoroughly reshaped the quality of his faith:

> The referential pole of his life continues to be the Father. He continues to have confidence in him, but now that confidence finds nothing in which to root. It becomes a confidence or trust against trust. Jesus's prayer in the garden of Gethsemane does not presuppose the same conception of God that Jesus had at the start of his life. Fidelity to the Father now stands in the presence, not of the Father's imminent coming, but of Jesus's imminent death. And Jesus sees his death as the death of his cause. Letting God remain God now lacks any verification; it is done in the absence of any verification at all.[2]

The Death of Jesus as a Trinitarian Event

Moltmann has pointed out that we cannot do adequate justice to the death of Jesus unless we interpret it on three levels: the religious, the political and the theological.[3]

On the religious level, for example, Jesus's death is a confrontation with Judaism. It is of utmost significance that Jesus was rejected by the official leaders of Judaism as a blasphemer. He did not die a martyr's death, the death of a hero, such as did the Maccabees.

But as St Paul says, he died an accursed death, since he was hung upon a tree. (Gal. 3:13). The Letter to the Hebrews expresses this fact dramatically when it speaks of Jesus being killed outside the gate (Heb. 13:12), that is, not in the holy city of Jerusalem but as one cast out and rejected. Jesus's whole life was a confrontation with the official religion of his day and his harshest words were reserved for so-called religious people. Thus St Paul says that the death of Jesus forces us to choose: salvation in the law (i.e. the religion of Judaism) or salvation in the cross. (Rom. 10:4).

Also on the political level, the death of Jesus is a confrontation between two sources of authority, that of Caesar and that of Christ. This confrontation is portrayed most dramatically in the trial scene, where Jesus confronts Pilate face-to-face. Pilate believes himself to be the ultimate authority over Jesus and condemns him to death. But for those who have faith, the resurrection of Jesus means that Pilate's power was illusory. The ultimate source of authority is Jesus. God governs the world through his Lordship. This is particularly important because Jesus has revised the meaning of power in terms of service. All master–slave relationships have been turned on their heads. Jesus the Lord became the servant of all. He no longer calls his disciples servants but friends and gives the new commandment: 'You know that those who are supposed to rule over the Gentiles lord it over them, and their great men exercise power over them. But it shall not be so among you; but whoever would be great among you must be your servant and whoever would be first among you must be the slave of all.' (Mk. 10:42–44). This teaching is especially important in view of the history of Christendom. As Moltmann and others such as E. Peterson[4] have shown, there has been a dangerous tendency for the church to identify itself with political power. In the early Middle Ages, Jesus was often portrayed in art according to the image of the Emperor. To be sure, Jesus is Lord but he is risen Lord always bearing the wounds of the passion in his body as a reminder that he rules from the cross. Thus the Lordship of Jesus is a constant challenge to our human assumptions about power. For the Christian, there is no power but only the charism of authority exercised as a service. Hence the cross of Jesus stands as a permanent obstacle to any easy alliance between church and state. Christ's church living under the sign of the cross has always the vocation to exercise a critical role *vis-á-vis* secular power. Naturally the same criterion holds for the exercise of power within the Christian community.

However, Jesus's contestation of the Jewish religion and of political authority pales in significance in comparison with the greatest confrontation of the cross, i.e. the confrontation of all our ideas about God. Indeed one could go further and say that the cross is an event between God and God. As we shall explain, the cross is an event in which we see an abyss in the divine life, a division between God and God (*Nemo contra Deum sive Deus ipse*), a separation, however, which is also bridged over by God, so that we must affirm: God is love.

It seems impossible to find a way to by-pass the New Testament testimony that in the passion Jesus experienced an impenetrable darkness. All the gospels testify to the fact that Jesus experienced a dread and an anguish of soul in the garden of Gethsemane. According to Mark, precisely at this moment Jesus calls God Abba, and begs that his Father remove this cup of suffering. (Mk. 14:32). But his prayer remains unanswered. Again the earliest account of Jesus's death on the cross testifies that he died with a loud cry and called out, 'My God, my God, why hast thou forsaken me?' (Mk. 15:34). When we note how the other evangelists modify this word from the cross, we can be fairly certain that the cry from the cross was one of the clearest memories of the first communities. Thus the God with whom Jesus lived in the intimate trust of a child did not rescue him from this dark night. Leander Keck observes, 'Jesus died without a word or a wink from God to reassure him that, whatever the gawking crowd might think, he knew that Jesus was not only innocent but valid where it mattered.'[5] Continuing this reflection Keck says that such a death involves a crisis in our understanding of God, both for Jesus and for us. Jesus assured us that God is trustworthy, that he is faithful to himself and his work, that he will bring about the Kingdom, that we can abandon ourselves to him with utmost confidence. Yet this God does not save Jesus from death. Nor does the Kingdom come. What comes is only the cry of dereliction on the cross. Hence if this God is proved trustworthy, nonetheless he is a God who shatters our expectations. As Keck says, 'The only God who is trustworthy is the One who does not interfere to protect the pious but who is present in the thick darkness, perhaps even as thick darkness.'[6]

However, such reflections do not as yet take us to the heart of the mystery of the cross. We arrive at this centre only when we see this event as an event between the Father and the Son, an event between God and God, an event, in other words, involving the whole Trinity. It is perhaps St Paul who draws out the full implications of the cross as a trinitarian event. First of all, according to Paul, the cross is an event involving the double surrender both of the Father and the Son. In Romans (8:32), Paul says that God did not spare his own Son but gave him up for us all. Likewise in Galatians (2:20), Paul speaks of 'the Son of God who loved me and gave himself for me'. In both cases the Greek word is *paradidonai* which means to 'hand over'. What does this handing over imply? If we take seriously the darkness and the cry of abandonment on the cross, it would seem that the handing over is a handing over to God-forsakenness. As Moltmann stresses,[7] the cross is an event of a double God-forsakenness. The Son finds himself abandoned by the Father, handed over to death. And the Father who hands him over suffers the death of the Son. In this moment of the cross, the divine being is rent asunder. Father and Son are held apart by death, darkness and sin.

A number of points of clarification seem to be called for. First of all, this God-forsakenness can be further determined by another verse of St Paul: 'God made him who knew no sin to be sin so that we might become the righteousness of God.' (2 Cor. 5:21). Here again we have a dramatic assertion. On the cross the Son is made sin, is identified with our condition of sinfulness. Balthasar and others have pointed out how difficult it has been for the church to accept such statements with full seriousness. For example, in the soteriology of Anselm, Jesus suffers the punishment of sin, but is not touched by the reality of sin as such in his own being. But if we accept fully what Paul affirms, we must say that Jesus experienced God-forsakenness on the cross, for that is what sin is, separation from God. In other words, on the cross Jesus experienced the reality of hell.

Secondly, I have said that the cross shatters our ideas of God. The cross forces us to confront one of the deepest of all theological problems, God's suffering. Under the influence of Greek philosophy, Christian theology has tended to affirm that God is impassible. However, the whole tradition of the Old Testament speaks rather of the pathos of God for his people. The cross is the culmination of this tradition. Here God literally takes suffering into his own life. In this century, theologians such as Barth have shown that the cross shatters all such axioms as God's impassibility. However, a theologian such as Moltmann goes even further. We must not only think theistically of a God who suffers but as Christians we must think in a trinitarian way.[8] We must ask not only what the suffering of the cross means for the Son but we must also ask what it means for the Father. Moltmann affirms that it would be impossible to maintain that the Father's heart is unaffected by the death of his Son. The Father suffers the loss of his Son. Hence the cross involves not only the passion of the Son but also the passion of the Father.

Let us, however, return for a moment to this concept *paradidonai*. We have already noted that the cross involves a mutual surrender of Father and Son. A number of contemporary theologians such as Moltmann and Balthasar[9] cite the reflection of Popkes who maintains that the word *paradidonai* must not be watered down to mean 'send' or 'give'. It must be taken in the strongest possible sense to mean 'hand over' or 'deliver up'. Popkes compares what happened on the cross to what happened between Abraham and Isaac. But whereas God relented in the case of Abraham's sacrifice of his son, he did not relent in the case of Jesus. Popkes even goes so far as to say that we can speak of the first person of the Trinity casting out and annihilating the second.

Such an interpretation seems to me to be mistaken for several reasons. First of all, it places such an emphasis on the action of the Father that it overlooks the fact that according to the New Testament there is always a mutual *paradidonai*. The Father's surrendering of his Son is matched by the Son's obedience and surrender of himself out of love for us. The full implications of this mutual surrender can only be fully grasped when we penetrate to the heart of the trinitarian mystery. First of all, it is critical to see that the Son in his very being is obedience. And this obedience is not just an alien, heteronomous obedience but it is precisely the obedience of Sonship. The New Testament constantly returns to the theme that Jesus's Sonship consists in his obedience. 'I do always the things that are pleasing to him.' (Jn. 8:30). What Jesus can do in his absolute freedom is always determined by his being the Son. As Balthasar notes, what could be *de potentia absoluta* is not possible *de potentia trinitaria*, namely that the Son would transgress the realm of his mission.[10]

This fact reminds us that the mission of Jesus which is fulfilled in the cross has its origins in the eternal Trinity. If we conceive of the event of the cross as a divine drama involving the Father and the Son, then as Balthasar argues, this drama must be grounded in the eternal trinitarian drama of the divine life.[11] The cross is the working out in history of the drama, which surpasses every drama, namely the eternal dramatic action within God himself. In other words, the only way to avoid seeing the cross as the imposition of an alien obedience is to situate the dramatic action of the cross within the eternal trinitarian drama. This is the merit of Balthasar's trinitarian theology. Balthasar wants to stress that the cross is a separation of Father and Son, but the dramatic caesura that rends the heart of God on Calvary has already been embraced from all eternity by the divine Trinity. For from eternity the Father has given himself away to the Son, has risked his being on the Son, and from eternity the Son has been a yes to the Father, a surrender of obedience. Thus the Father's risk of himself on the Son creates a space for the Son. The Father separates himself from himself, so that the Son can be. But this separation is also bridged over in eternity by the Holy Spirit, the communion of the love of the Father and the Son. Hence according to Balthasar, there is both a separation and a union within the divine life which makes possible the separation and the union of the cross-event. The dramatic action of the economic Trinity is made possible and embraced within the primordial drama of the eternal Trinity. Thus Balthasar locates the drama between God and the world within the drama between God and God:

In the emptying of the Father's heart in the begetting of the Son, every possible drama between God and the world is already included and indeed surpassed, since every world can only have its place within the difference between the Father and the Son, a difference which is both held open and bridged over by the Spirit.[12]

Drawing out the consequences of this doctrine for the event of the cross, Balthasar continues:

That God as Father can so give away his divinity, that God as Son does not merely receive it as lent but possesses it as being essentially equal, expresses such an ungraspable and unsurpassable 'separation' of God from himself, that every other separation (which indeed the primordial separation makes possible), even if the darkest and most bitter, can only happen within it.[13]

Therefore, the conclusion of our reflections thus far is that the most profound hermeneutic of the cross is a properly theological one, that the cross can only be grasped adequately if it is seen as an event between God and God, between the Father and the Son, an event which is the working out in history of a primordial drama between the Father and the Son who from eternity risk their being on one another, who are thus distinct but yet one in the Holy Spirit who is their bond of communion.

From the Theology of Good Friday to the Theology of Holy Saturday

To understand more fully the meaning of Jesus's death, it can be helpful to reflect on the human phenomenon of death. From the anthropological point of view we can see that death has both an active and a passive dimension. Every death, for example, is a manifestation of human freedom. Death is the ultimate possibility of my human existence, the act by which I render the project of my life complete. A human being does not die like an animal, but is always challenged to take a stance toward his death. My death can be an act of trust, a surrender of love or it can be an act of bitterness, rebellion and resignation. No outside person or force can determine how I die. In this perspective, we see the significance of the New Testament affirmation that Jesus's death represented an active self-surrender. His death was a sacrifice. Thus in the gospel of Mark, Jesus says, 'The Son of Man did not come to be served but to serve and to give his life as a ransom for many.' (Mk. 10:45). Along the same lines, the Jesus of the fourth gospel affirms, 'I lay down my life, that I may take it again. No one takes it from me, but I lay it down of my own accord.' (Jn. 10:17–18). Perhaps we could call this aspect of the paschal mystery the theology of Good Friday.

However, an anthropological reflection reveals another dimension of death, death as a passivity. Philosophically, one can say that death is never merely an act of freedom but is also a threat, something that I suffer and undergo, my ultimate limit and fate. In this sense, human death reveals all of human life as questionable. Death raises the question whether human life is ultimately a frustration, whether it is possible to find an ultimate fulfilment and sense to life. From a theological point of view we can say more. Death is experienced as a threat, precisely because of the link between death and sin. The human being dies not only a natural death but the death of a sinner. Death represents the concretization of the human dread of being cut off from ultimate fulfilment. In theological terms, death represents the possibility of being cut off from God, that is, the possibility of hell.

This passive dimension of death is represented by the theology of Holy Saturday. Here we are indebted to the reflections of Hans Urs von Balthasar[14] who in turn incorporated this dimension of the passion of Jesus into his theology on the basis of the mystical experiences of his friend Adrienne von Speyr. What does Balthasar want to affirm in his theology of Holy Saturday?

At least in two places in the New Testament (1 Peter 3:19; 4:6), there are references to Jesus's descent into hell. According to Balthasar, this picture of the descent into hell is clearly mythological but it contains a fact of the deepest theological importance. For Balthasar, the descent of Jesus into hell is not a triumphant journey of the victorious Christ into the underworld. To be sure, the victory of the resurrection has its effects even there and has a retroactive power for all who preceded Christ in history. But Jesus's journey into the underworld is his total identification with us in our condition of powerlessness as sinners.

To draw out the implications of this identification, Balthasar appeals to the Old Testament picture of Sheol. Sheol, which is the state of the dead, is a constant theme of the psalms. Various metaphors are used to describe it: it is the land of darkness (Ps. 49:19) and of silence (Ps. 94:17), a place from which there is no return (Job 7:9). It is described as the Pit and the eternal prison (Ps. 30:9; 88:6); the dead are isolated, cut off from God (Ps. 6:5) and from the world above, lacking in all strength and vitality (Ps. 88:4), they are mere dust (Ps. 30:9).

But when the New Testament says that Jesus 'became sin' (2 Cor. 5:21) and when it speaks of his journey to the underworld, the biblical writers are wanting to affirm that Jesus embraced our death of sin.

On the cross, Jesus too was separated from the Father. Jesus became lifeless and could not raise himself from the dead. On the cross God's Word became silenced. On the cross Jesus experienced a radical aloneness, an utter passivity. As Balthasar puts it, he even became a cadaver obedience.

If as we said above, the death of a sinner is hell, if God's holiness excludes the sinner from his presence, because his holiness cannot abide sin, if sin must provoke the wrath of God, then Jesus on the cross experienced hell. As Balthasar says, hell is in fact a christological concept. The meaning of hell is determined from Christ's experience on the cross. In the Old Testament, hell was only foreshadowed because all who lived before Christ lived in the hope of his coming. The light of his advent shone in the Old Testament period. Only in the moment of the cross is this light cast out of the world. Only in this moment does the death of God become a serious possibility. But because Jesus is risen and because he has suffered hell in our place, no one of us is ever destined to know the weight of sin as he did. He has removed from us the fate of hell. This is our consolation. The one who will judge us is the one who has been judged in our place. As the fourth gospel puts it, 'The Father judges no one, but has given all judgment to the Son.' (5:22). But as St Paul asks, 'Who is to condemn? Is it Christ Jesus who died (for our sakes) and who intercedes for us?' (Rom. 8:34). Because Jesus experienced the ultimate aloneness of hell, none of us is destined for this isolation, but we are always destined for companionship with him. As Paul also says in the Letter to the Romans, 'If we live, we live to the Lord; and if we die, we die to the Lord; so then, whether we live or whether we die, we are the Lord's.' (14:8).

There is one final aspect of this theology of Holy Saturday, the mystery of human freedom. As Barth once noted, sin is the impossible possibility. God in creating us takes a risk on our freedom. God exposes himself to the possibility of an ultimate No. The mystery of this possibility of a No seems to confront us with a dilemma. If the human being with his or her freedom can resist God to the end, it would seem that God's purposes are thwarted and the human person possesses an ultimate sovereignty over God. On the other hand, if God's desire to save overpowers human freedom, it seems that the human being has been robbed of the very quality which makes him human. Balthasar finds the resolution of this seeming cul-de-sac in the mystery of the cross. God allows the human person really to be free, God accepts the human No, but in his infinite mercy and with the ingenuity of the divine intelligence, finds the appropriate solution by deciding to accompany the human liberty into the most extreme space of its final isolation. Hence the sinner finds himself no longer ultimately alone but in the company of the God-forsaken Son of God. God breaks into his solitude and accompanies the human person into the most extreme situation of his negative choice so that the sinner finds himself in a situation of co-solitude (*Mit-Einsamkeit*). As Balthasar writes:

> Into this finality (of death) the dead Son descends, no longer acting in any way, but stripped by the cross of every power and initiative of his own, as one purely to be used, debased to mere matter, with a fully indifferent (corpse) obedience, incapable of any active solidarity – only thus is he right for any 'sermon' to the dead. He is (out of an ultimate love however) dead together with them. And exactly in that way he disturbs the absolute loneliness striven for by the sinner: the sinner, who wants to be 'damned' apart from God, finds God again in his loneliness, but God in the absolute weakness of love who unfathomably in the period of nontime enters into solidarity with those damning themselves.[15]

Trinity and Atonement

St John speaks of Jesus as the Lamb of God who takes away the sin of the world. (Jn. 1:29). In the classical theology and spirituality of the church, Jesus has borne our sin in such a way that he has expiated our sinfulness and made atonement to the Father. Today such ideas have often come under attack. Especially the theory of St Anselm, the so-called satisfaction theory, has often been attacked on the grounds that we can no longer think of the cross as appeasing the justice of an angry God. Many modern writers such as Rahner have stressed that the cross-event is the result of the Father's love and not an event which wins back the Father's love.

Although I would thoroughly agree that God is from all eternity forgiving love and that it is this love which motivates the Incarnation and the cross, I would disagree with the idea that one can dispense with the tradition of atonement. For although God is always disposed to forgive, we must ask how God can forgive in a way which takes seriously both the reality of sin and the reality of human freedom.

According to Norbert Hoffmann, the understanding of atonement in the Old Testament is dramatic.[16] God enters into true partnership with his people in the covenant. When Israel sins, God remains true to his covenant fidelity but also true to respecting the freedom of his covenant partner. The way in which God can forgive and still take this freedom seriously is atonement. In the act of atonement God lets the person experience the reality of sin for what it is, namely separation from God. Sin is the absence of God. Sin is incompatible with God and therefore God casts it out of his life. In expiating sin, the sinner turns back to God but experiences his separation as suffering, and by suffering the loss of God, the sinner transforms his sin into love. Hence atonement is not a matter of suffering an extrinsic punishment of God. Atonement is facing the reality of sin for what it is.

This Old Testament background provides the key for understanding the cross as atonement. First of all, it is important to see that God's goal in creating the world was always christological. Jesus Christ is not an afterthought to the act of creation. As the Letter to the Ephesians says, 'God chose us in him before the foundation of the world.' (1:4). Hence our place in God's eternal purposes is christological. In this context sin is not just a moral failure or the breaking of a commandment. Sin is the refusal of Sonship in Christ. Sin is the human No to Sonship in the Son. With this No, sin which should not have a place usurps the place of the Son.

But in the cross God hands over his Son to bear our sin. The Son in his freedom bears the entire weight of what sin is. He who is sinless knows and becomes sin. This explains the agony of the cross and the cry of dereliction. He faces the abyss of sin, of separation from God. He drinks this cup to the dregs but because he does so out of love, he transforms sin into love, he displaces the sin and recreates the condition of Sonship. As Hoffman writes:

The love which here bears sin, turns this sin into a pain which can be appropriately described with only one word: hell. But because hell is suffered by such a love, it is suffered to death. Hell exists here only as the suffering of this love, it is nothing other than love in the form of suffering, the pain of the Son, who is deprived of the Father: 'My God, my God, why hast thou forsaken me?'[17]

Hence Jesus suffers hell in our place. In this sense, he represents us. He confronts the power of sin and overcomes it through suffering love. We are then inserted into his Sonship anew. That is why Paul can say that we are a new creation. Here we see the theology of the *admirabile commercium*. Jesus becomes what we are (sin) so that we can become what he is (righteousness). In the words of 2 Corinthians (5:21), 'God made him who knew no sin to be sin, so that we might become the righteousness of God.'

Balthasar notes that God is always forgiveness. God does not have to change his mind. Thus he observes that in the cross-event God is not reconciled to the world but rather the world is reconciled to God. Hence we can see the process of creation and reconciliation in this way: (1) We are created in the Son. (2) Sin is the No to the offer of divine Sonship. Sin usurps the place of the Son. (3) On the cross Jesus takes the place of sin. He carries the weight of sin. But in bearing this sin in suffering love, he transforms it. The cross is the negation of the negation. (4) Finally, by means of this expiation, we are restored to our sonship in Christ. The paschal mystery makes possible a new creation.

It is important to see that such an act of divine forgiveness, which takes seriously the freedom of God's covenant partners, is only possible in a trinitarian understanding of God. God's revelation in Christ shows us that he is God for us. But the cross lets us see how radical is the quality of this 'for us'. The God of neo-Platonic philosophy was unaffected and untouched by the suffering of the world. We Christians, on the other hand, affirm that sin touches the Father's heart. God is so much 'for us' that he does not put a limit on his love even in the face of the reality of sin. He takes sin into his own life. But this is only possible because God is the love of the Father and the Son. The love of the Father and the Son is, in the words of Adrienne von Speyr, 'wide enough to embrace the whole world'. The world finds its place in this space opened up by the Father's self-gift. But because God is this open community, in which the Father is totally for the Son, and the Son totally for the Father, the decision becomes possible whereby the Father sends the Son into the far country and the Son in free obedience accepts the mission to identify with us even to the point of the abandonment of the cross. God so desires the response of his creation that in order to overcome the refusal of his offer of love he sends his Son into the darkness of the cross. Hence the soteriological 'for us' of the cross is grounded in the unbounded selflessness of the divine persons who are in their being for one another.

The Bond of Love

In this chapter we have usually spoken of the cross-event as an event between the Father and the Son. At the same time we have constantly referred to the paschal mystery as a trinitarian event. The unspoken third member without whom the cross is unthinkable as an event of revelation is the Holy Spirit. The Holy Spirit is the neglected member of the Trinity and his presence is often only hinted at, such as when the author of the Letter to the Hebrews says, 'Christ through the eternal Spirit offered himself without blemish to God.' (Heb. 9:14).[18] Nevertheless the presence of the Spirit is indispensable. We have stressed the God-forsakenness of the cross, the mutual abandonment of the Father and the Son. However, the resurrection reveals that in fact even in the moment of their extreme separation, they were united. The bond which united Father and Son on the cross was the Holy Spirit. We have also seen that the cross was an act of divine forgiving love on the part of the Father and of divine suffering love on the part of the Son. Thus the bond of love uniting Father and Son in this moment of dereliction was the Spirit of their union. This also follows from what we saw about the presuppositions for the economic Trinity. The separation of Father and Son in the cross is grounded, as we saw, in the separation of Father and Son in their eternal life, a separation however which is held open and bridged over by the Spirit. Also in the cross, the moment of their separation is paradoxically their moment of most intense union.

An important consequence follows from this. In the inner-trinitarian life we noted that the love of Father and Son was not closed in upon itself. The Holy Spirit opens the divine life outward to creation and reconciliation. The Holy Spirit completes the circle of the divine life but it is not a closed circle but an open one. In the same way, from the event of the cross, from the event in which God totally identifies himself with forsaken humanity, the Spirit is poured forth upon the world, the Spirit of healing and reconciliation. As Moltmann puts it, 'Out of this happening between the Father and the Son the surrender itself emerges, the Spirit which accepts the forsaken, justifies the godless and makes the dead alive.'[19]

This outpouring of the Spirit and the essential link of the Spirit with the cross has important implications for Christian spirituality and praxis. Here it could suffice to say that the gift of the Spirit, poured out from the cross, grounds the Christian spirituality of compassion. We have seen that the entire theology of the Old Covenant is based on the pathos of God. In the New Covenant this pathos is not understood dialogically as an I–Thou relation but triunely as the compassion of the Father, the Son and the Holy Spirit. The suffering and sin of the world touch the divine heart, so that the three persons of the Trinity involve themselves in our suffering and redeem it. On the basis of such a vision of God the only legitimate Christian response is a spirituality of compassion. The Christian is summoned not to withdrawal from the world but to overcome the threat of apathy and, like God, to open himself or herself to the suffering of his brothers and sisters. The key word in Christian spirituality is identification. Since God has identified himself with the poor and the abandoned in the cross of Christ, the Christian wants to place himself where God has placed himself. As St Ignatius Loyola proposes in the *Spiritual Exercises* (see no. 167), the more one grows in love, the more one chooses the form God himself has chosen: poverty, humiliations, insults. It is a Christian choice motivated by an identification of love. But it is not a choice merely oriented to the past. Rather the Spirit, poured out from the cross, drives the contemporary believer to an identification of compassion with the contemporary Christ, with the Christ who has identified himself with the God-forsaken, and who therefore can and must be found hidden under the form of his poor and suffering brothers and sisters.

The Name of God

In the First Letter of St John, the disciple gives God the name of love which must guide every Christian reflection (see 1 John 4:16).

In contrast to the God of the philosophers, whether it be the Unmoved Mover of Aristotle or the Absolute Subject of Hegel, St John tells us that God is love. Such an affirmation is not a statement of reason; it is a way of recapitulating our Christian experience of God. The God we believe in is the God whom we have come to know in Jesus Christ. But the culmination of our experience of Jesus is his cross and paschal mystery. That there is a God who can so go out of himself that he exposes himself to sin and dereliction, that there is a God who is Lord only by being servant of all is something scandalous to reason and even to the religious instinct. As Paul says, the cross is inevitably 'a stumbling block to Jews and folly to Gentiles' (1 Cor. 1:23). However, the cross understood as the conspiracy of the love of the Father, the Son and the Holy Spirit impels us to see the truth of the dictum of St Anselm: God is *id quo maius cogitari nequit*, that than which a greater cannot be thought. The *Deus semper maior*, however, whom we discover in the cross cannot be adequately described as Absolute Being but more aptly deserves the description coined by John Wesley, Pure Unbounded Love.

V

God the Holy Spirit

Introduction

In the history of Christian theology, the Holy Spirit has often appeared as the unknown God. From an historical perspective, the nature of the Holy Spirit was not a subject of speculative interest until the fourth century. A theologian of the Eastern Orthodox tradition, Vladimir Lossky, interprets this fact theologically,[1] arguing that in the Incarnation the person of the Son is clearly manifested whereas in the coming of the Holy Spirit the Person of the Holy Spirit remains undisclosed. In the Incarnation, the divine nature hides itself under the form of a slave. Nevertheless Jesus as God's Incarnation reveals the human face of God. In the bestowal of the divine gift of deification, however, the Holy Spirit annihilates herself so to speak losing herself in the work of sanctifying the human person.[2] (The reader will notice that I use the feminine pronoun for the Holy Spirit. The reasons for this usage are explained in the last section of the present chapter.)

Nevertheless, the recognition of the mission of the Holy Spirit to sanctify and to divinize, a mission which has its highest expression in baptism, reveals the need to clarify the nature of the Holy Spirit. The historical impulse to reflect upon the person of the Holy Spirit was soteriological. If God wishes to save the human being, if baptism is the beginning of a process of sharing God's own life, then what is the nature of the Holy Spirit who makes this divinization of the creature possible?

These questions became pressing ones for the church in the fourth century. After the Council of Nicaea in which the church definitively rejected Arianism and affirmed that the Son was fully equal to the Father, the church was called upon to clarify its understanding of the nature of the Holy Spirit and the relation of the Spirit to the Father and the Son.

The first important contribution was made by Athanasius who was also the champion of the full divinity of the Logos. In regard to the Incarnation, Athanasius had argued that since only God can save, Jesus must be fully divine. Using the same argument, Athanasius reasoned that since the purpose of the Incarnation was our divinization, the Holy Spirit who makes Christ present within us, must also be fully God in the same sense as the Father and the Son. What the Son is by nature, we are by participation. But the condition of possibility of this participation is the Holy Spirit. Hence the Holy Spirit is divine. In a famous text, Athanasius wrote:

> The Holy Spirit is the ointment and the seal with which the Word anoints and signs everything ... Every time we say that we are partakers of Christ and partakers of God, we mean that that unction and that seal which is in us is not of a created nature, but is of the Son, who joins us to the Father by the Spirit who is in him. If the Holy Spirit were a creature, there could be no communion of God with us through him. On the contrary, we would be joined to a creature, and we would be foreign to the divine nature, as having nothing in common with it.[3]

Under the influence of Athanasius and the development of his basic insight by the Cappadocians, the Council of Constantinople in 381 proclaimed, 'We believe in the Holy Spirit, the Lord and Giver of life who proceeds from the Father, who together with the Father and the Son is adored and glorified.' A careful reading of this confession of faith reveals that here the Holy Spirit is not defined in explicit terms to be divine. The word *theos* is not used for the Spirit, nor is the controversial word 'consubstantial' which had caused such a furore when applied to the Logos by the Council of Nicaea. Instead the Council Fathers concentrate on the mission of the Holy Spirit, her soteriological role. The Holy Spirit is the life-giver. This implies that the Spirit shares in the work of God as creator. Only God can call into being from nothing. Moreover, the life which God offers is not just the life of the creature, but as we have seen, the supernatural life of grace. This work is here attributed to the Holy Spirit. Since the Holy Spirit has the task of deifying the creature who has been called into being, the Spirit is worthy of the divine title, Kyrios or Lord, along with the Father and the Son. Moreover, in this brief formula, the Council points theology in the direction of worship. The proclamation of the Spirit's divinity and Lordship is not just an abstract affirmation – it is oriented to praise. The Holy Spirit is worthy of adoration and glorification. The goal of theological statements is doxology.

The Identity of the Holy Spirit

In spite of the elusive nature of the Holy Spirit, can we gain some insight into her identity? This question has haunted theologians down the centuries. Without pretending that I can offer a definitive Christian answer to this question, I would like to appeal to two insights which form a central motif in the vision of St Augustine and have continued to recur through the centuries, namely the Spirit as gift and the Spirit as love.

Let us look for a moment at the identity of the Holy Spirit as the gift of God. This image has a firm foundation in the Bible. A favourite text of St Augustine is that of Romans (5:5)[4] where St Paul speaks of the 'love of God which has been poured into our hearts by the Holy Spirit who has been given to us.' Another text to which Augustine appeals is chapter 4 of St John, the dialogue of Jesus with the Samaritan woman. The woman asks for ordinary water but Jesus admonishes her, 'If only you knew the gift of God, you would ask for living water.' Later, in chapter 7, the evangelist speaks of streams of living water which shall flow from the believer and he identifies this living water with the Holy Spirit (Jn. 7:39). Another important text for Augustine is Acts 8:20, the story of Simon the magician, who wants to buy the powers of the Holy Spirit from the Apostles. Peter reproaches him scornfully for 'thinking God's gift is for sale.' Finally, Augustine appeals to Hebrews (6:4) where the author speaks of the enlightenment which believers receive 'when they have had a taste of the heavenly gift and a share in the Holy Spirit.'

Augustine, ever a master of language, is able to use the fecundity of the Latin language to theological effectiveness by employing the image of the *donum Dei*. The Holy Spirit is as such God's gift. What God gives is nothing less than himself. As Rahner would put it, the Giver and the Gift are identical. The Holy Spirit is also what has been given, the *donatum*. The Holy Spirit indicates as well that God in his very being is sheer giftedness, that is, God is *donabile*. God's being implies the capacity to give himself away. Rahner, in his magisterial work *Foundations of Christian Faith*, appropriates the Augustinian image and speaks of the Giver, the Gift and the condition of possibility of accepting the Gift.[5] All three can be identified with the Holy Spirit. God wants to give not something different from himself. He wants to bestow himself as Gift. This gift allows the believer to participate in God's own life. However, the elevation of the creature to share the divine life exceeds the capacity of the believer. Faith as the existential participation in God's offer of himself must itself be the work of grace. The Holy Spirit is the enabler of faith; hence as Rahner says, the Holy Spirit is the condition of possibility of our accepting the gift.

In this sense we can speak of the Holy Spirit as the subjective aspect of revelation. Because of the Holy Spirit, God's revelation does not confront us as an object over against us. God's revelation happens in us. We become the event of revelation. In Rahner's language, the human subject becomes the event of the loving self-communication of God. God so enters into union with the creature, that human subjectivity itself becomes the event of revelation. There is a mysterious identity between the revealer and the revealed in the act of revelation. Rahner expresses this truth by saying that God the Holy Spirit becomes a co-constitutive element of human subjectivity.[6]

This subjective dimension of the revelation-event has been well expressed by Kilian McDonnell when he speaks of the Holy Spirit as the light which enables the believer to see Christ. Unless we dwell in this light the eye is blind and fails to grasp Christ as the revelation of God. In another image, McDonnell speaks of the Holy Spirit as the proportionality which both allows us to know the revelation-event and enables us to be conformed to it. He writes, 'With the proportionality which the Spirit gives, one can know Jesus, the image of the Father who sent him. With the same proportionality one can recognize the presence of God in history and the face of the Son in his church.'[7] Therefore, one can say that the Holy Spirit has both a noetic and an ontological function. Epistemologically, she lets Christ be recognized. Ontologically, she forms Christ in the depths of the person who believes.

The other important image used by Augustine is that of love. In a famous analogy of the divine life, one later exploited by Richard of St Victor, Augustine says that there are three in the Trinity: the lover, the beloved and the love itself.[8] According to this model of understanding the divine life, the Father is the lover who gives himself wholly to the Son. The Son is the beloved, the perfect response to the Father's offer. The Holy Spirit is the bond of their love. Augustine returns to this image numerous times in the *De*

Trinitate and in one place refers to the Holy Spirit as the ineffable communion of the Father and the Son.[9]

This model has been a formative one in the Western tradition of Christianity. The Western conception of the divine life is that of a circle. The Holy Spirit completes the circle so that there are no further processions in God. With the Holy Spirit the circle of love finds its fulfilment. At the same time, it would be a mistake to see the divine love as closed in upon itself. For the Holy Spirit not only perfects the divine love but is the opening of the divine love outward to the world, to time and to history. Moltmann speaks of the divine life as an open circle.[10] Kasper, in this context, speaks of the Holy Spirit as the divine ecstasy – etymologically speaking, the divine being's standing outside itself. Kasper writes, the Spirit 'expresses the innermost nature of God – God as self-communicating love – in such a way that this innermost reality proves at the same time to be the outermost, that is, the possibility and reality of God's being outside of himself. The Spirit is, as it were, the ecstasy of God; he is God as pure abundance, God as the overflow of love and grace.'[11]

These insights of Moltmann and Kasper are not altogether new. Even in the Middle Ages, Richard of St Victor recognized that a love closed in upon itself is no genuine love. According to Richard, friendship, in order to be true love, requires a third. The two must move beyond themselves in openness to a new reality. Thus Richard referred to the Holy Spirit as the common beloved (*condilectus*) of the Father and the Son. The ideas of Richard of St Victor have been brilliantly developed today by the Catholic theologians, Heribert Mühlen and Hans Urs von Balthasar.[12] Both point to the marriage covenant as the prime analogate for the trinitarian life. The love of husband and wife contains a fruitfulness which neither of them suspected, a fruitfulness which becomes concrete in their child. The child is neither the child of the father alone nor of the mother alone but is *their* child, the fruit of their union. Here we seen concretely in human experience the superabundant, overflowing character of love which has its ultimate origin in the trinitarian life.

Mühlen, basing his theology of the Holy Spirit explicitly on the theology of Richard of St Victor, argues that in human experience, there are three primordial words: I, Thou and We. The We is not merely the sum of the other two. The We often has a certain independent character of its own. Again this is seen most clearly in the marriage covenant. The marriage covenant is not just my marriage or your marriage but *our* marriage. The content has an objectivity in the sense that it is a reality which transcends the two who have entered into it. On the basis of this analogy. Mühlen suggests that we understand the Holy Spirit as the divine We, as the We-in-person of the trinitarian life. In this sense the Holy Spirit is pure relationality. The identity of the Holy Spirit is defined in terms of relation to the Father and the Son. The Holy Spirit has nothing of her own but is wholly referred beyond herself to the Father and the Son. Within this conceptual scheme, Mühlen suggests as a definition of the Holy Spirit that the Spirit is one person in many persons. The Holy Spirit is person by being the bond, the relation of the Father and the Son. One can only identify the person of the Spirit by reference to the other two persons without whom the Holy Spirit cannot be a person.

Jesus Christ and the Spirit

We have already seen that the Spirit can be described as God's ecstasy, the opening of God outward to creation and history. The Spirit is thus the clue to the universality of God's desire to save. At the same time Christianity is centred on a particular saving event which bears the name Jesus Christ. As Kasper says, in Jesus Christ the deepest and the final Mystery of all reality has become unveiled in a totally unique, underivable, unrepeatable and unsurpassable way. How can we put together these two convictions of faith, the universality of God's saving designs and the particularity of the revelation-event in Jesus Christ? This is one of Christian theology's deepest conundrums.

If we look at the biblical testimony to Jesus, we see that one of the first Christian attempts to solve this problem was to confess him as the man filled with the fullness of the Spirit. The Spirit of God which was always at work in creation and in the history of Israel, which was given partially to the prophets, came to dwell in Jesus in eschatological fullness. In this way Jesus does not drop from heaven as an unexpected saviour but is seen as the fulfilment of a long process of preparation.

We have already seen (Chapter III) that no aspect of the life of Jesus is neglected by the biblical writers in their desire to link Jesus's mission and his possession of the Spirit. From his virginal conception to his resurrection from the dead Jesus is understood as one operating out of the fullness of the possession of the Spirit. As Acts 10:38 sums it up, 'God had anointed him with the Holy Spirit and power and because God was with him, he went about doing good and healing all who had fallen into the power of the devil.'

Philip Rosato, in an article on Spirit-Christology, points out that there are clearly many advantages for the church to rediscover this perspective.[13] First of all, here is a christology which is firmly biblical in character and links Christ to the Spirit of Yahweh who is active in the history of his people. He notes that the person of Jesus is set into a larger framework – that of the spiritual, federal and political concept of the Spirit of Yahweh who was active in the history of the judges, the kings and the prophets of the Old Covenant. Secondly, this christology focuses on the eschatological significance of Jesus for all men and women. It overcomes an individualistic type of piety and links Jesus to the human hope for a kingdom of justice and peace. Finally, it clearly places the accent on the human need for redemption. This christology is soteriological to the core. The being of Jesus cannot be understood in isolation from his mission in history.

In spite of these advantages, the Spirit-christology of the Bible practically died out in the church. The reason seems to be primarily an historical one. The Ebionites, an heretical sect mentioned as early as the second century, regarded Jesus as the new Moses. The Spirit of God which had been given to Moses now came to rest forever on Jesus. The Ebionites placed great emphasis on the baptism as the moment in which Jesus, the human person, received the anointing of the Spirit. Clearly this interpretation of Jesus was adoptionistic. Jesus in his being was a mere man on whom the Spirit of God came to rest. The church could not accept this interpretation of Jesus, for it clearly contradicted another biblical motif, that of the Word made flesh. If Spirit-christology stressed the pneuma-sarx relationship, the incarnational christology accentuated the logos-sarx identity of Jesus. The incarnational christology highlighted the ontological identity of Jesus as a divine person made flesh in the Incarnation. Although this is a non-negotiable truth of faith, it can be argued that the concentration on this understanding of Christ to the exclusion of other biblical dimensions obscured the full meaning of Jesus Christ as God's revelation. In particular, the neglect of the pneumatological understanding of Christ in favour of an ontological christology led to a christology which was abstract, individualistic, particularistic and a-historical. It is interesting, for example, that the classical definition of Chalcedon so concentrates on defining the being of Jesus that it by-passes his concrete history.

Nonetheless we might ask ourselves if a return to a pneumatological christology today leads to obscuring the singularity of Jesus and his unique ontological identity. Do we run the risk of a new adoptionism? Does the reemergence of Spirit-christology open us to the charge that in this understanding of Jesus, he is different from us only in degree and not in kind?

Many theologians today would argue that it is possible to combine these two biblical models, the Spirit model and the incarnational one. Kasper,[14] for example, argues that the Bible contains a unique and universal setting into which Jesus can be placed without doing violence to his ontological singularity. According to Kasper, the Spirit is the appropriate category to mediate between God's inner life and his work *ad extra*. The Spirit prepares the creation for the Incarnation, guides Jesus during his earthly life and through the glorification of the Son opens up the real possibility for all men and women to share in the love-intention of the triune God.

In addition to Kasper, it is perhaps Mühlen who has done the most to reinvigorate Spirit-christology and to show its compatibility with the classical Logos-christology of the church. The critical question is the relationship between Incarnation and anointing of the Spirit. We have seen that the Ebionites believed that Jesus was a mere man who was anointed with the Spirit at the moment of his baptism. Mühlen rejects this and argues that Jesus was anointed with the Holy Spirit from the first moment of his incarnate life. For Mühlen, the baptism is an important event in the life of Jesus in which he becomes more conscious of his identity and mission, but he has the fullness of the Spirit from the first moment of his human existence. An important point here is the relation of person and nature. In the Incarnation the divine person takes on a human nature. But we have seen that according to Mühlen the Holy Spirit is always a relation of person to person. In this perspective Mühlen argues that the anointing of Jesus with the Spirit logically presupposes the Incarnation. Temporally the Incarnation and the anointing are co-terminous but ontologically the anointing presupposes the Incarnation. The Holy Spirit comes to dwell in the person of the incarnate Christ. From the first moment of his existence Jesus has the fullness of the Spirit. However, as Mühlen also notes, this fullness is given to him for the sake of his mission. The grace of the Head is for the sake of the members.

How does the Holy Spirit function in the life of Jesus? Here we can appeal to two insights, one of von Balthasar and one of Mühlen. Balthasar develops the idea of what he calls a soteriological inversion of roles in the immanent and economic Trinity.[15] In the life of the immanent Trinity, the Father and the Son breathe the Holy Spirit. Hence the Spirit is wholly receptive, passive – formed by their mutual self-giving. But in the work of the economy of salvation, the Holy Spirit becomes active and the Son passive. The Incarnation happens when the Spirit overshadows the Virgin Mary. The Son lets himself become incarnate. During the earthly life of Jesus the Father manifests his will to the Son through the inspirations of the Spirit. The Son in obedience responds to the Spirit's impulses. The culmination of this obedience is the cross. With the resurrection, however, the Son resumes his active role. He pours out the Spirit on the church. The Spirit in the community is always bound to Christ. The Spirit always has christological form.

The other insight as to the function of the Spirit during the life of Jesus comes from Mühlen who stresses the role of the Holy Spirit as *vinculum amoris* and bond of unity. As we have seen, it is the Spirit's task to unite. The Spirit is ontologically one person in many persons. Thus during the earthly life of Jesus the Spirit continues to link the Son to the Father. The culmination of this mission takes place on the cross where the Spirit preserves the unity of the God-forsaken Christ and the surrendering Father even in the moment of their most extreme separation.

Finally, we might return to the question of the universality of the Trinity's love-intention and the particularity of the Christ-event. Philip Rosato suggests that we can view the action of the Spirit as two spiralling cones which meet in the resurrection.[16] God's searching love in history manifests itself through the Spirit. The Spirit is God's offer of himself in time. This offer which is co-terminous with the whole of history reaches its culmination in the Christ-event where Jesus responds perfectly to the Father's offer. As St Paul says, 'Jesus was always Yes to the Father. In him God's Yes to the world finds its perfect response.' (See 2 Cor. 1:19). This Yes which is accepted by the Father in the resurrection overflows in the eschatological outpouring of the Holy Spirit at Pentecost. The grace which Christ possessed in its fullness is made available to his members. Thus through the Holy Spirit, God's love now becomes a gathering love leading the whole creation back to the Father. The goal of history will be reached when Christ hands over the Kingdom to the Father and God will be all in all. If, to use Moltmann's phrase, we look at the trinitarian history of God and God's trinitarian relationship to the world, we notice diverse patterns for the period of preparation, for the fullness of time in the Christ-event and for the period of the church.[17] In the Old Testament, the Father gives his Spirit to Israel, the Spirit who speaks through the prophets and prepares for the coming of the Son. In this period of preparation one can visualize the Trinity's relation to the world in this way: Father → Spirit → Son. With the incarnation, the relationships change. Here the Father sends his only-begotten Son, who in the fulfilment of his mission sends the Spirit at Pentecost. An image of God's dealings with the world in the fullness of time would be: Father → Son → Spirit. With the beginning of the period of the church, a new pattern is established. Here the Spirit has the priority, continuing the work of Christ, leading the world to glorify the Son, so that through the Son, creation can be led back to the Father. In the eschaton, God's trinitarian relations with the world will be complete. In the end-time, the Father will be passive, receiving everything through the Son in the Spirit. The end-time will be the glorification of the Trinity, God will be all in all, God in the world and the world in God. The model for this relationship will be: Spirit → Son → Father. Hence the plan of God's love-intention can be seen as a great circle of exodus and return. Everything comes from the Father and returns to him.

The Holy Spirit in the Church

We have already seen the role of the Holy Spirit in the life of the Trinity and in the life of Jesus. Let us now continue our reflection by examining the role of the Holy Spirit in the life of the church and of the individual Christian.

In order to try to do justice to the mystery of the church, it is essential to refer to the christological and to the pneumatological aspects of her being. St Paul highlighted the christological dimension when he referred to the church as the body of Christ. The Second Vatican Council, taking up this idea, affirmed that the reality of the church is analogous to that of the incarnate Word. 'Just as the assumed nature inseparably united to the divine Word serves him as a living instrument of salvation, so, in a similar way, does the communal structure of the church serve Christ's Spirit, who vivifies it by way of building up the body (cf. Eph. 4:16).'[18]

Many commentators have seen in this explanation of the Council an understanding of the church as a sacrament. Underlying the idea is the affirmation that Jesus Christ is the primordial sacrament of God. God in his own reality is hidden but it is the mission of the Son to reveal him. The whole life of Jesus, his words and deeds, in fact, his whole human reality is revelatory of the Father. As Jesus says in the fourth gospel, 'He who sees me sees the Father.' (Jn. 14:9). Jesus is a sacrament, because he is a finite visible reality which makes present and tangible in history the invisible reality of God. In the same way, the church makes Christ present in the world. Although Christ has been taken from our sight at the Ascension, his presence still makes itself felt in the world through his community. When the Christian community lives the new life of faith, hope and love which Christ makes possible, his presence becomes visible in the world. Also, in the church's permanent structures such as the scriptures and the sacraments, Christ's mission is extended in space and time. When the church truly lives its mission from Christ, when the church lives what it is by its deepest union with its Lord, a light shines out in the world which is a mediation of God's presence in Christ and so the church's being as sacrament is a mediation which renders faith possible. Men and women see in her a reality which draws them to God.

The Second Vatican Council spoke here of an analogy between the church and the incarnate Word. In the preceding paragraph I have tried to highlight the similarities. At the same time it is always important to be aware of the dissimilarities in any analogy. According to the model of the Mystical Body, the church is a prolongation of the Incarnation. This analogy limps, however, because of the sinfulness of the church. The church is not united to Christ by a new hypostatic union. Thus there is a danger in this model of deifying the church, and Protestants are wary of this model precisely because of this tendency. As a church made up of erring and sinful members, the church is always summoned, as Vatican II also admitted, to a continual purification. Another limit of the christological emphasis is that the church tends to be so identified with its institutional elements such as the sacraments, ordained ministries and teaching office that the freedom of the Spirit to blow where she will is domesticated if not extinguished.

Therefore, it seems essential, if a balanced view of the church is to be maintained, to complement the christological conception of the church with a pneumatological one. An important stimulus along these lines can also be found in Vatican II's teaching on the church. The Council Fathers write:

> In order that we may be unceasingly renewed in him, he has shared with us his Spirit, who, existing as one and the same being in the head and in the members, vivifies, unifies and moves the whole body. This he does in such a way that his work could be compared by the holy Fathers with the function which the soul fulfils in the human body, whose principle of life the soul is. (no. 7).

In his magisterial work *Una Mystica Persona*,[19] Mühlen has appropriated this perspective to develop a profoundly pneumatological understanding of the church. Aware of the limitations of the analogy of the church and the incarnate Word, Mühlen has suggested that we not think of the church as the prolongation of the Incarnation but rather as a prolongation of Christ's anointing with the Spirit. The central insight of Mühlen that the Holy Spirit is one person in many persons can be fruitfully applied here and can link together the articles of faith on the Trinity, christology and ecclesiology. We have already seen that the person of the Holy Spirit is the bond of unity linking the incarnate Christ to the Father. We have also seen that the anointing of Jesus with the Spirit is an anointing which is co-terminous with the Incarnation. But, as Mühlen constantly emphasizes, the grace of the Head exists for the sake of the members. Hence the fullness of grace which Jesus possessed was showered upon the church in the paschal mystery. The church is a pneumatological event born in the event of the cross and resurrection. Today many authors recognize that it would be too simplistic to locate the founding of the church explicitly in the ministry of Jesus, although it is prepared there, for example, in the choosing of the twelve as the leaders of the new Israel. Likewise many theologians would prefer to reappropriate the patristic tradition of locating the founding of the church in the cross-event. On Good Friday, we are told that blood and water flowed from the side of Christ. The Fathers of the church saw in this event a symbolic expression of baptism and eucharist. On Easter night, Jesus appeared to the disciples, breathed on them and said, 'Receive the Holy Spirit.' Lossky points out[20] that in the Eastern Orthodox tradition the breathing of the Spirit on Easter night is considered the first communication of the Spirit, when the Spirit is handed over to the whole church that is, to the church as the body of Christ. This event is complemented by the second bestowal of the Spirit, made on Pentecost Sunday, when the Spirit is bestowed on individuals. According to Lossky these two outpourings of the Spirit are complementary. By the first the church becomes the body of Christ. This giving of the Spirit renders the church a stable edifice built upon a firm foundation (see Eph. 2:20–22). The bestowal of the Spirit to individuals is, by contrast, dynamic. It guides believers on their pilgrim way toward full divinization in the Kingdom of God.

To return now to Mühlen's theology of the church, his definition of the Spirit as one person in many persons provides the basis for a pneumatological vision of the church. Here as always the mission of the Holy Spirit is to create unity. Mühlen can say that the church is one mystical person because the bond of unity between Christ and each believer as well as the ground of unity among believers themselves is the same Holy Spirit. As we have seen, the Holy Spirit is always a relation of person to person. Whether in the Trinity, in the Incarnation or in the church, the Holy Spirit does not unite person to nature but person to person. Hence in the church the Spirit does not enter into a new hypostatic union. There is only one hypostatic union, that of the divine person of Jesus Christ and the human nature. In the church the Spirit unites the person of Christ to the person of each believer. At the same time the ground of unity among members of the Mystical Body is the same Spirit. Thus in the language of *Lumen Gentium* (no. 7), the Holy Spirit is the soul animating the Mystical Body. Mühlen's vision gives us a truly theological understanding of the unity of the church rather than a sociological one. The unity of the church is not based ultimately on the free decision of the members of the church to belong to it. The church is not like a club to which human beings freely decide to belong. Membership in the church is in the last analysis not an option of human beings from below. The existence of the church is from above, from Christ's choice and election of us. And the source of our unity is not the free choice of the members but the person of the Holy Spirit dwelling both in Christ and in us. As the Council insists, there is one and the same Spirit in the Head and in the members. Hence to grasp the church as one Mystical Person is to see that the bond of unity in the church is so deep, that in spite of the manifold diversity of its members, the unity is greater than the diversity, for the unity is nothing less than the bond of unity of the Trinity itself, the person of the Holy Spirit.

The Holy Spirit in the Life of the Believer

To complete our reflection upon the economy of the Holy Spirit, let us return to the indwelling of the Holy Spirit in each individual believer. The divinization of the creature is one of the main themes of the history of Christian theology, a motif especially beloved in the Eastern Orthodox tradition. The goal of God's trinitarian relations with the world is to make us partakers of the divine nature. Here is the recurring motif of the *admirabile commercium*: God has become what we are, that we might become what he is. What Christ is by nature, we are by grace.

Certainly this conviction is a central one in the New Testament. At the last supper, Jesus promises that he and the Father will come to make their abode in the believer. 'If any man loves me, he will keep my word, and my Father will love him, and we will come to him and make our home with him.' (Jn. 14:23). The same idea is stressed by St Paul. The Apostle teaches that the believer is a temple of the Holy Spirit. Rebuking the Corinthians, St Paul asks rhetorically: 'Do you not know that your body is a temple of the Holy Spirit within you, which you have from God?' (1 Cor. 6:19; see also 1 Cor. 3:16).

How should we understand this indwelling of the Holy Spirit? I believe that there are two extremes which we should avoid. The first is that of the Eastern Orthodox theologian, Gregory Palamas.

Gregory follows the apophatic tradition of the East which distinguishes the essence of God from his self-communication. He appropriates the tradition of Maximus the Confessor who maintains that 'God is communicable in what he imparts to us: but he is not communicable in the incommunicability of his essence.'[21] Gregory develops the theory of the distinction between God's essence and his energies. The energies are not creatures, they are uncreated manifestations of God's being but they are distinct from the divine essence. According to Gregory, we are divinized because the divine energies dwell in the creature. The Holy Spirit as such does not indwell the believer but only the divine energy. The logical conclusion of this position, however, is that God as such is not communicated to the creature. Thus we could ask, on this position, if we are really saved. As Kasper notes, the question which arises from the radical negative theology of the Palamite is whether his doctrine does not make the immanent Trinity irrelevant to the history of salvation and deprive it of any role therein.[22]

The other extreme is represented by the tradition of neo-scholastic theology which argued for only an appropriated indwelling of the Holy Spirit in the soul. For this theology, since the work of God *ad extra* is indivisible, we must speak of a general indwelling of the Trinity in the soul but not of a personal indwelling of the Holy Spirit. Although I would agree that all the persons of the Trinity are involved in the economy of salvation, I would also want to affirm that they are involved according to a definite order.

Thus I would argue for a personal indwelling of the Holy Spirit in each believer. The grace of divinization which is given to each believer in baptism is in the first instance uncreated grace, that is, the Holy Spirit herself. Because the Holy Spirit is in the believer, the believer is immediately united with Christ. United with Christ, the believer is enabled to go to the Father through the mediation of Jesus. Hence we go to the Father through the Son in the Holy Spirit.

The tradition of neo-scholastic theology is often accused of reifying grace. There is undoubtedly some truth in this charge. Neo-scholasticism tended to take created grace as the prime analogate of grace. We have opted on the other hand for uncreated grace as the prime analogate. Nevertheless created grace is important but as a preparation for uncreated grace and as its immediate consequence. The presence of the Holy Spirit necessarily makes itself felt in the effects it works in the life of the believer and in the life of the community. Perhaps a more contemporary word for these created graces is charism.

St Paul seems to have presupposed that a Christian community indwelt by the Holy Spirit would be a charismatic community. In his communities, there was no lack of created gifts to manifest the presence of the Spirit. Among them he mentions speaking in tongues, teaching, healing, prophecies. The early centuries of Christianity seem to have expected such gifts, but as the church became more institutionalized, the charisms were often usurped by the prescribed offices of the community. Although eruptions of charismatic activity have been a recurring phenomenon in the history of the church, the Catholic community, at least in recent centuries, has tended to be very suspicious of charisms and charismatic people who seemed to threaten the institutional stability of the church. At the Second Vatican Council, when the question of charisms came to be discussed, many bishops felt that genuine charisms were an extraordinary phenomenon which were rarely given to the church. This view, however, was emphatically rejected by the Council and in a revolutionary passage in *Lumen Gentium*, the Council Fathers declared that it is of the nature of the church to be charismatic. According to Vatican II, there will always be a healthy dialectic between charism and institution in the church. The Fathers state:

> It is not only through the sacraments and official ministries that the Holy Spirit sanctifies and leads the People of God and enriches it with virtues. Granting his gifts 'to each one as he chooses', (1 Cor. 12:11) he also distributes special graces among the faithful of every rank, by which he makes them able and willing to undertake various tasks or services advantageous for the renewal and upbuilding of the church, according to the words of the Apostle: 'To each is given the manifestation of the Spirit for a useful purpose.' (1 Cor. 12:7). These charisms, whether they be the more unusual or the more simple and widely diffused, are to be received with thanksgiving and with consolation, for they are exceedingly suitable and useful for the needs of the church. (no. 12).

Perhaps the most striking idea in the preceding definition is that

God distributes his gifts to the faithful of every rank. Hence it can be expected that each of the faithful has some created grace, some gift or charism as a result of the indwelling of the Holy Spirit. The other important idea in Vatican II's understanding of charism is the link between the gift received and its usefulness for building up the community. Summing up Vatican II's understanding of charism, Francis Sullivan writes, 'A charism can be described as a grace-given capacity and willingness for some kind of service that contributes to the renewal and upbuilding of the church.'[23] Granted then that everyone has some charism and that charisms are given for service, we ought to ask how these charismatic elements are to be related to the institutional structures of the church. Is the institutional dimension of the church a degeneration of the charismatic, a reality that one must make sense of sociologically rather than theologically, or is the church as institution also the work of the Holy Spirit?

Charism and Institution

We suggested above that the institutional and charismatic elements in the church must be understood dialectically. One can verify this truth concretely in the life of the community. Although special gifts and charismatic leaders emerge unpredictably in the history of the church, the charismatic is nourished by such institutional and stable elements as the sacred scriptures and the sacraments. At the same time the institutional offices of the community are intrinsically related to the charismatic. A person to be ordained, for example, must manifest evidence that the Lord is calling him to this service in the community and that the Spirit has bestowed on him the gifts necessary for fulfilling his ministry. Moreover, as many theologians have argued, one of the tasks of the office-holder in the community is precisely to promote the charisms of the various members of the church, to co-ordinate them and to harmonize them for the common good. In addition, as Balthasar has noted, the life of the office-holder as a representative of Christ, only makes sense insofar as the office-holder conforms himself to the Lord, literally takes on christological form. According to Balthasar, this form is characterized by the obedience which culminated in the self-offering of the cross.[24] The pastor of the community whose identity is most clearly expressed in the eucharist must live out the mystery which he celebrates. As the bishop exhorts the candidates in the ordination ritual: *imitamini quod tractatis.* Seen in this light, the mission of office in the community must be, in Balthasar's words, a crystallization of love.[25]

Reflecting on this dialectical tension between charism and institution theologically, we can see that the basis for the tension is not just sociological but is rooted in the divine mystery itself. First of all, we have seen that God always deals with his people through the two missions of the Son and the Spirit. The tension between the institutional and the charismatic reflects the dialectic of the christological and pneumatological poles of Christian experience. This polarity is constantly reflected in the writings of the New Testament, for example, in the letters of St Paul. Paul recognizes the outpouring of pneumatic gifts upon the newly born Christian church. But these gifts must be ordered christologically. The Corinthians, for example, have a superabundance of gifts but they have forgotten the mystery of the cross and resurrection. Thus Paul can warn that exaltation of the gifts without reference to Christ and his paschal mystery is self-destruction. The Apostle writes, 'No one speaking by the Spirit of God ever says, "Jesus be cursed!"' However he goes on to add that the work of the Spirit consists precisely in leading the believer to confess the Lordship of Jesus (1 Cor. 12:3). Hence the christological and the pneumatological form an intrinsic unity. Therefore, Josef Ratzinger believes that a critical development within the early Christian community was precisely the christological transformation of pneumatology.[26]

One interpretation of the nature of the Christian community is that the christological grounds the institutional and the pneumatological grounds the charismatic. The Spirit pours out gifts on all. Each has a gift for the up-building of the whole. At the same time Christ pledges never to abandon his church. Within the church there is a guarantee of Christ's eschatological victory. This guarantee is expressed in a certain pre-given objectivity which confronts the individual believer. As expressions of this objectivity one could mention the sacraments with their *ex opere operato* efficacy, the sacred scripture with its promise of God's address, the teaching office with its guarantee of infallibility, the office-holder with his representative function.

However, it is possible to pursue this reflection even more deeply and see the tension between the institutional and the charismatic as rooted in the person and mission of the Holy Spirit herself. It is Balthasar who has pursued this line of reflection most fruitfully. If we look to the inner life of the Trinity, we see that the Holy Spirit is totally receptive *vis-à-vis* the Father and the Son. The Holy Spirit is breathed forth as the fruit of their love. In this sense the Holy Spirit is 'normed' or 'objectified' by them. The Holy Spirit has nothing of her own but is totally referred to the Father and the Son. According to Balthasar, this quality of being normed is the ultimate theological foundation of everything institutional in the church.[27] And indeed here in the inner life of the Trinity we can see why the criterion for the discernment of spirits will always be christological. The reason is that the Spirit is always the Spirit of the Father and of the Son and hence is always bound to them. Nevertheless this is only one side of the truth. For we have also seen that the Spirit is the ecstasy of God. The Spirit is the overflowing fruitfulness of the love of the Father and of the Son. Hence the Holy Spirit represents the freedom of God, the incalculable creativity of the divine activity. In Balthasar's words, the Holy Spirit is the 'determining form of freedom'.[28] The Spirit is freedom (cf. 2 Cor. 3:17), the personified freedom of the Father and of the Son. Hence the institutional will never be able to express adequately the trinitarian purposes of God for the world. The Spirit will always transcend the barriers of the institutional. For it is the Spirit's mission to be ever creative, to interpret the meaning of the Christ-event to the world in ever unpredictable ways. Hence the Christian community does not live in slavish imitation of Christ or in a petrified repetition of the past. The Spirit is future-oriented. According to Balthasar the great signs of the Spirit's presence in the church are the saints, the representatives of holiness whom God gives the church in each new age. These saints with their unique missions represent what the Spirit is doing in the church and saying to the world at any given moment of history. They have their unique *kairos* which cannot be domesticated by the institutional church. Thus, however repressive the institutional element of the church may become, the living sign of her vitality is the presence of the saints who are so full of the Spirit that the institution can never repress their God-given charisms.

According to this vision of Balthasar's, the church is inevitably a tension of institutional and charismatic elements which, though they may be in tension, can never ultimately be in contradiction. An ultimate contradiction is impossible, for the tension is rooted in the divine life of the Trinity itself where the Spirit is ever bound to the Son (institutional) yet at the same time always beyond him (charismatic). The Holy Spirit as the objectified love of the Father and the Son has a mission which is full of tension, a tension however which is not destructive but creative. For as Balthasar says, the Spirit as formed freedom is at one and the same time 'determining-institutionalizing' and 'liberating-universalizing'. Only in a trinitarian understanding of the Spirit can one resolve the seeming contradiction at the heart of Christian faith, the paradox of universality and particularity.

One Faith – Different Theologies

The theology of the Holy Spirit provides us with a splendid example of the distinction between the unity of faith and the pluriformity of theologies. The development of pneumatology in the East and in the West is analogous to the emergence of diverse conceptual models in the physical sciences such as the particle and wave models employed to explain the phenomenon of light. As Congar notes, each theological tradition has its own inner logic. Each is impossible in the categories and vocabulary of the other.[29] Writing along the same lines, Kasper affirms that there is a common ground of faith as attested in scripture and tradition but differences in terms of images and concepts.[30]

The chief protagonist in the West was no doubt Augustine. Augustine employs a circular image for understanding the role of the Holy Spirit in the Trinity. The Spirit, proceeding from the Father and the Son, is the fruit of their love and the completion of the inner-trinitarian life. Augustine gives a priority to the divine nature over the three persons and hence gives less prominence to the monarchy of the Father than the Greeks do. Augustine also stresses the psychological analogies based on the human soul, according to which the Logos is the *verbum mentis* of the Father. This tradition will find its full flowering in Aquinas who understands the processions of the Son and the Spirit as acts of intellect and will.

The East developed its theology of the Holy Spirit under different impulses. The sources lay in Athanasius and the Cappadocians. According to Congar, the main points of the Greek tradition are the following: the difference between the divine substance and the divine hypostases, the monarchy of the Father, the distinction between the begetting of the Son and the proceeding of the Holy Spirit, the reference of the Spirit to the Son, because the Spirit proceeds from the Father through the Son and rests in the Son and is the Son's image and expression.[31]

A point of supreme importance for the East is the monarchy of the Father. He is the origin of everything in the Trinity. Lossky stresses as well the apophatic character of the Eastern mystical tradition.[32] Hence it is impossible to fathom the nature of the three hypostases. We simply know on the basis of revelation that there are three but we do not know how. Finally, it is worth noting that the East never appropriated Augustine's notion of the interior word. The East stresses the exterior word. According to St John Damascene the Holy Spirit is likened to the breath 'which accompanies the Word and makes it effective.'[33] The Spirit 'proceeds from the Father and rests in the Word and reveals him.' Thus whereas in the West theologians used a circular model, in the East they employed a linear one. The Spirit proceeds from the Father through the Son.

If one compares these two theological traditions, one can see that there are corresponding strengths and weaknesses in both. The strength of the Western tradition is that it clearly brings out the relationship between the Son and the Spirit. Since the Spirit is always the Spirit of Christ in the economy of salvation, the same must hold in the divine life. Otherwise the correspondence between the economic and the immanent Trinity is dissolved. At the same time there is a danger in the Western model due to the priority it gives to the divine nature over the monarchy of the Father. This can lead to an abstract conception of God and to the separation of the philosophical doctrine of God from the real God whom faith confesses, that is, the Father, the Son and the Holy Spirit. Theologians like Lossky see in this tradition the tendency toward Christomonism whose consequences are also felt in ecclesiology. A strongly christocentric theology leads to a strongly authoritarian ecclesiology (the Pope, for example, as the Vicar of Christ) which can stifle the freedom of the Spirit. While admitting these dangers, it is important to acknowledge that Western theology has not been totally unaware of them. Thus, for example, even Augustine stressed that the Spirit proceeds *principaliter* from the Father,[34] and to overcome the East's fear about compromising the divine unity, the Latin tradition taught that the Spirit proceeds from the Father and the Son as from one principle.[35]

As we might expect, the strengths of the East correspond to the weaknesses of the West. The principle advantages of Eastern theologians lie in their stress on the monarchy of the Father, in their recognition that *ho theos* in the Bible in the first instance means God the Father. Likewise the East emphasizes the freedom of the Spirit and hence develops a more charismatic view of the church and a more universalist perspective as regards the economy of salvation. At the same time, the chief weakness of the East is its failure to clarify the relation of the Son and the Spirit. The Son must not be absent from the procession of the Holy Spirit if the Spirit is always the Spirit of the Son in the economy of salvation.

From a practical point of view, the tragedy of our Christian history is that the diversity of these two rich traditions led to the schism of the church. Naturally, the sociology of knowledge would also point out that political factors played a significant, if not the decisive, role in the split. Today the ecumenical task of the church confronts at least two questions: first, the practical one of whether the *filioque* should be left in the creed as a requirement of faith, and secondly, the theological task of deepening our understanding of the relation of the Son and the Spirit. As to the practical problem, there seems to be no impediment to dropping the *filioque* from the creed. It is clearly recognized today that the *filioque* was not part of the Nicene-Constantinopolitan Creed and was indeed added to the Creed centuries later by a unilateral action of the Pope. Hence it would be permissible to drop it. On the other hand, the way forward may be to accept a legitimate diversity, and thus for Western Christians to continue to use it while recognizing the legitimacy of Eastern Christianity's refusal to do so.

As to the theological task, further reflection on the relation of the Son and the Spirit is critical. As Kasper notes, 'The issue here is not a useless quarrel about words but a deeper understanding of our salvation, that is, the question of how the salvation effected by Jesus Christ is communicated through the Holy Spirit.[36] As I mentioned above, the critical question is the nature of the presence of the Son in the procession of the Spirit. A valuable contribution to this discussion has been made by Moltmann.[37] Moltmann appeals to Epiphanius who taught that the Holy Spirit proceeds from the Father and receives from the Son. What does the Spirit receive from the Son? Moltmann answers: form or *Gestalt*. This accords with the Eastern idea that the Spirit rests in the Son and is the image of the Son. For this reason the Holy Spirit makes the Son known in the economy of salvation. According to this approach, we could say that as regards hypostasis the Spirit is from the Father (*ek tou patros*), but as regards her form, she receives from the Son. If one wanted to express the unity of faith in a dogmatic formula, a possible suggestion would be to revive the ancient tradition according to which the Holy Spirit proceeds from the Father through the Son. Another possibility would be that suggested by Moltmann: I believe in the Spirit of the Son who proceeds from the Father and receives her form from the Son.[38]

The Femininity of the Spirit

Under the critique of feminist theology and the charge of the patriarchalization of the gospel, the question of the femininity of God has been raised again with a new urgency. In a joint study with his wife Elizabeth, Jürgen Moltmann has suggested[39] that the fatherhood of God must be complemented by the affirmation of the divine motherhood. The ultimate source of the Godhead is not merely a Father-principle, for the first person of the Trinity not only begets the Son but also bears the Son in his womb. Hence the origin of the Godhead is both masculine and feminine. God is not only our heavenly Father but also our divine Mother.

Other theologians have preferred to explore the feminine dimension of God with reference to the Holy Spirit. In *The Divine Mother*, Donald Gelpi develops a theology of the Holy Spirit in terms of the femininity of God. Working out a complex theory of the Trinity largely in terms of process categories, Gelpi develops the idea of the Spirit as the divine mind, the lure of feeling in God and the source of divine evaluation.[40]

Naturally, there is a significant biblical basis to undergird this conception, namely that of the Old Testament tradition of *sophia* or divine wisdom, a feminine term and concept which has often been linked to the Spirit. In addition to wisdom, there is the other Old Testament category of *ruach* or the breath of God which is feminine and which has traditionally been associated with the Spirit. On the other hand, as Congar points out, it is difficult to justify the femininity of the Spirit on linguistic grounds alone, since if one appeals to ancient languages, one must admit that whereas *ruach* in Hebrew is feminine, *spiritus* in Latin is masculine, and *pneuma* in Greek is neuter.[41]

Nevertheless, there do seem to me to be several important theological reasons for associating the Spirit with the feminine dimension in God. First of all, we have seen that the Holy Spirit is pure receptivity *vis-à-vis* the Father and the Son. The Spirit is in her being sheer gift. Moreover, the Spirit is the fruitfulness of their love, a fruitfulness which overflows in the creation and in the economy of salvation.

The nineteenth-century Catholic theologian Scheeben[42] further developed this aspect of the Spirit by pointing out the analogy between Adam and Eve on the one hand and Christ and the church on the other. Eve was directly created from the side of Adam. The church is the new Eve created out of the side of Christ. Many patristic theologians saw the birth of the church as taking place in the cross-event. On the cross Jesus breathed forth the Spirit (Jn. 19:30), the Spirit who gives birth to the church. This is symbolized dramatically in the flow of water and blood from the side of Christ. The mother church under the power of the Spirit gives eternal life to her children in the waters of baptism.

Moreover, especially from the perspective of the cross-event, there is a parallel between Mary and the church. Mary's role in salvation history is her radical Yes to God's plan to offer himself as gift to the world. Mary's *fiat* reverses the refusal of Eve to obey God's design. In Mary's surrender of obedience she becomes the New Eve. In the moment of her final letting go of her son on the cross, Jesus gives her to be the mother of the new community which has its birth from his open side. Hence the link between Mary and the church. The church formed by the Spirit is in its very being Marian and feminine. The church exists as church when it relives Mary's surrender to the Word. Through this obedience of faith the church also gives birth to the Mystical Body of Christ.

In this chapter, we have seen how God's dealings with the world always involve the two missions of the Son and the Spirit. In terms of christology, Jesus is the Spirit-filled person. In terms of the church as well there is always a christological and a pneumatological dimension. These could be seen as the church's masculine and feminine dimensions.[43] Christ who is masculine is the Lord of the church. But he stands over against the feminine-Marian church who is the bride. This church, perfectly exemplified in Mary, is fashioned by the Spirit poured out from the cross to be the immaculate bride spotless and without wrinkle (Eph. 5:27). All persons in the church, whether male or female, are led by the feminine Spirit of God to fulfil their Marian-feminine vocation of receptivity toward God's gift, of surrendering to God's offer by which the Word comes to birth in the depths of their being and overflows in graced fruitfulness for the world.

VI

The Concept of Person in Trinitarian Theology

The Origin of 'person' in Christian Theology

The traditional formula which the non-professional believer has learned to express his faith in the Trinity is 'one God in three persons'. Having tried to anchor our Christian faith in the triune God in our experience of the economy of salvation, it is now time to investigate this classical formula in more detail, to ask ourselves what it means and whether it is still a useful formula for Christians today.

A glance at the history of Christian theology reveals that the formula is not so obvious as might appear and that the term 'person' did not make a gentle entrance into theology. The early centuries of Christian faith were a time in which the great doctrines of the church were given conceptual clarification under pressure from deviating tendencies inspired from various concerns. Two of the major problems of these early centuries were subordinationism and modalism. First, the church had to clarify the relation between Jesus and the Father, i.e. the God of the Old Testament, and subsequently the relationship between the Spirit, the Logos and the source of the Godhead. The great achievement of the Councils of Nicaea and Constantinople was to affirm the co-equality of the three in the face of a Hellenistic philosophy which sought to subordinate Son and Spirit to the Father, rendering them in fact less than divine. One of the major obstacles to the definition of the co-equality of the three was the fear of modalism, that is, the doctrine that God appears to be three but in his own life is a bare monad. The Fathers of Nicaea, for example, feared that the introduction of the term *homoousios* (consubstantial) to express the equality of the Logos and the Father would lend support to the modalists. They took the step, nonetheless, because they could find no other way to reject Arius's subordinationism.

The problem then arose as to how to preserve the diversity of the three. The Cappadocians were the first to suggest a way out of the impasse, coining the formula: one *ousia*, three *hypostases*. The term *hypostasis* stressed the concrete objectivity of the three. God exists in three objective manners of presentation. They were also the first to hint at the notion of relation as a way of distinguishing the three, although they were vague when trying to pinpoint more precisely the nature of the relations, suggesting such formulas as unbegotten, begotten and proceeding.

For those in the West, a decisive step came with the introduction of the term person to describe the three. Augustine had to face the problem how to translate the Greek phrase, one *ousia*, three *hypostases* into Latin. A literal translation of *hypostasis* would have been *substantia*. Augustine feared employing the term since it sounded too tritheistic. Thus he reluctantly appropriated the term person. He seems to have been afraid of this term because it suggested to him the idea of separate individuals. Nevertheless in a famous phrase, he notes that he uses the formula 'three persons' not to say what the three in God are but rather to avoid being silent altogether.[1]

Looking at the history of the medieval tradition, we see that under the pressure of the christological and trinitarian debates, the concept of person received philosophical attention for the first time. A decisive step was taken by Boethius when he defined person as an individual substance of a rational nature. This definition became foundational for the medieval tradition; however, the more one reflects upon it, the more problematical it seems, because Boethius identifies the person with individuality. As Josef Ratzinger points out, Boethius's categories are still those of substance.[2]

The key to breaking out of this framework is that of relation. An important figure to move beyond Boethius was Richard of St Victor. Richard based his thinking about the nature of the three in God on the biblical affirmation that God is love. Richard then employs a social doctrine of God. He offers as a definition of person an 'incommunicable existence of an intellectual nature'.[3] If we look at the word 'existence', we see that it is derived from the Latin word *ex-sistere*, i.e. to step outside of. The word 'existence' is rich in its connotations; 'sistere' indicates that the person has its being in itself and not in another. The person exists in and for himself. But the particle 'ex' indicates the relationship of origin by which the person is constituted. Hence Richard preserves the Boethian accent upon substantiality but he complements this idea with that of relationality. As Heribert Mühlen comments,[4] the person is constituted not only by his substantiality but also by the origin from which he has his being.

Thomas Aquinas, with all the shrewdness of a thinker of genius, begins his meditation on the meaning of person by appealing to Boethius's definition but the use which he makes of it reveals a significant modification of Boethius's thought.[5] For, whereas in Boethius, the stress is on substance, in Aquinas the accent is on relation. At the end of Aquinas's reflection, he defines the three persons of the Trinity as subsistent relations. The relations are subsistent because each person is identical with the divine essence. The stress on subsistence also preserves the original Greek notion of *hypostasis*, that is, an objective presentation of the Godhead. The stress on relation, however, indicates that each person is who he is precisely because he is related to the others. Thus, in Aquinas's theology, person has a double connotation: *esse in* and *esse ad*. Each person is subsistent in the Godhead and identical with the divine substance; at the same time one can only define the person by referring to the person's relationship to the other. In this sense, Moltmann is right when he says that person in trinitarian theology is not a generalizing concept but is unique.[6] What each of the three persons has is, as Richard of St Victor says, incommunicable, each is defined by its relation of origin.

The Problem Posed by Modern Philosophy

If we look at this classical period of Christian theology, we note that the understanding of person is in some ways more akin to what we would describe as objectivity than as subjectivity. Over against modalism, the Greek Fathers wanted to stress three objective presentations of the Godhead. The same accent on the otherness of the three is found in the ontological concept of subsistent relations.

The problem for contemporary believers has radically shifted, however, because of philosophical developments since the Enlightenment. Descartes was perhaps the first significant thinker to shift the accent from a cosmological point of view to an anthropological one, from objectivity to subjectivity. His centring of philosophy upon the 'I think' paved the way for modern theories of subjectivity. According to this philosophy the person is identical with self-consciousness. The person is an autonomous centre of action, disposing of self in freedom. In contemporary parlance, person is spontaneously identified as centre of consciousness and freedom. However, if we bring these pre-reflective categories to theology, we are immediately confronted with a problem. For if we say that God is one being in three persons, and if we understand by person centre of consciousness and freedom, then God becomes three centres of consciousness and there are three 'I think's in God. But such an understanding is obviously the same as tritheism.

Two modern giants in theology tackled this problem in their dogmatics and made an important suggestion toward finding a way out of this impasse. The first is Karl Barth. Because of the difficulties posed by modern philosophical preconceptions, Barth suggested the alternative formulation of three modes of being in God, a phrase which he said was more or less an exact equivalent of the ancient Greek term *tropos hyparxeos* (relation of origin). Thus Barth writes:

> The statement 'God is one in three modes of being, Father, Son and Holy Spirit' thus means that the one God, i.e. the one Lord, the one personal God is what he is, not in one mode only, but – we appeal in support simply to the result of our analysis of the biblical concept of revelation – in the mode of the Father, in the mode of the Son, in the mode of the Holy Spirit.[7]

Barth freely admits that he is not offering a speculative solution and indeed claims that none is possible, since the inner realm of the divine life always remains numinous and we can never penetrate the 'how' of the divine processions. We must content ourselves with knowing on the basis of revelation that there are three without knowing how. Still he believes that his suggestion clarifies the problem and removes philosophical and linguistic confusion.

Karl Rahner, from the Catholic side, moves in the same direction. Rahner is much more explicitly influenced by philosophy than is Barth and indeed thinks within the framework of German idealism. For Rahner there is a primordial identity between being and knowing, and levels of being can be measured by the depth of presence to self. The human being is defined by his self-presence, which however is a finite self-presence, thus a self-presence which questions itself and can only fulfil itself by going into the world. Finite self-presence is thus constituted by a self/world polarity.

Essential to Rahner's philosophical anthropology is the conviction that human subjectivity, aware of its finitude in every act, is a dynamic drive beyond the finite to the Infinite. Finite subjectivity for Rahner is implicitly aware of God in every act of knowing and willing. God is the term of finite subjectivity. Whereas finite subjectivity is a self-consciousness conditioned by the world, God is an infinite self-consciousness, fully present to self without any necessary mediations of otherness. God is the ultimate I, the ultimate self-consciousness, pure subjectivity.

Along the same lines as Barth, Rahner affirms that this absolute subjectivity exists in three distinct ways. Rahner, however, shifts the Barthian terminology in order to avoid any impression of modalism in the classical sense. Thus Rahner suggests the terminology of three distinct manners of subsisting; for Rahner there is only one divine consciousness which exists in a three-fold way.[8] Perhaps one could say that, for Rahner, God is one Person in three manners of being.

How are we to evaluate these suggestions of Barth and Rahner? There seems to be a fair consensus that even if this approach is theologically legitimate, it presents us with kerygmatic and pastoral problems. The trinitarian faith of the church is notoriously difficult for believers to grasp. If there are difficulties in the language of the three persons, it seems probable that there are more difficulties in the language of three modes of being. One can hardly imagine someone praying to a mode of being.

Secondly, there is the question of modalism. I cannot accept the idea that Rahner or Barth are modalists in the classical sense of Sabellius. Sabellius taught that God appeared as three-fold in the economy of salvation but was a bare monad in the divine life. Both Barth and Rahner insist explicitly on the correspondence between God in the economy of salvation and God in his immanent life. Thus the terminology may have a suspicious ring but the conception is not modalistic in the sense of Sabellius.

However, a deeper unease remains in that Barth and Rahner are failing to give adequate attention to a significant aspect of the tradition, namely to the aspect of reciprocity and relationship. Josef Ratzinger makes the point, for example, that we cannot think of God merely as an ultimate I. The ultimate reality is not a mere I over against the human Thou. This neglects the whole dimension of the We. However much Christianity retains the monotheism of the Old Testament, the last word is not (*contra* Augustine) on unity. For Christians, it is not enough to say with Plotinus that the ultimate is the One beyond all being. For Christians the ultimate is community. The One also includes the We. The Christian doctrine of God constrains us to think multiplicity within unity. Ratzinger writes, 'The Christian concept of God has in principle given identical dignity both to multiplicity and to unity. While for the ancients multiplicity appeared only as the dissolution of unity, for the Christian faith, which thinks in trinitarian terms, multiplicity possesses *a priori* the same dignity as unity.'[9]

An attack along the same lines has been launched by Moltmann. Moltmann sees in Rahner and Barth the triumph of modern idealism. He believes that their thinking has abandoned its Christian origin and has substituted for the Christian God the absolute subjectivity of Hegelian philosophy. But, according to Moltmann, such a concept does not offer a genuine understanding of person but rather a refined form of egoistic individualism. Moltmann sees in Barth's and Rahner's concept of God the modern bourgeois concept of the individual which has been so decisive in forming our contemporary experience of society. Moltmann writes, 'What Rahner calls "our secular use of the word person", has nothing in common with modern thinking about the concept of person. What he describes is actually extreme individualism: everyone is a self-possessing, self-disposing centre of action which sets itself apart from other persons.'[10] Hence Moltmann would argue that if we are going to re-think the concept of person for trinitarian theology we must look not to Kant and Hegel but to the modern personalist philosophers such as Buber, Ebner and Rosenzweig.

The other critical objection which Moltmann brings against Rahner and Barth is that their concept of the absolute subject leads to a repressive form of monarchianism.[11] The I–Thou relationship to which Barth appeals is the God-man relationship. God is the I, the human being is the Thou. But as Barth also stresses, his whole conception of the Trinity is rooted in the Lordship of God. God reveals himself as Lord in the three-fold mode of Father, Son and Holy Spirit. But this easily degenerates into an I–Thou relationship according to the master–slave pattern. The divine subject is the absolute Lord, the human subject the slave. In short, Moltmann accuses Barth and Rahner of a hidden form of theism in which the Lordship of God *vis-à-vis* his creatures easily becomes the master–slave relationship. In this situation the whole problematic of the modern philosophy of religion develops. The human subject to preserve his own centre of freedom throws off the yoke of divine subjectivity in order to realize his self-consciousness. Moltmann believes that this cul-de-sac can only be avoided by returning to our geniune Christian origins and a communitarian concept of God as persons in relation. This model would offer the hope of grounding human community in divine community.

The Social Image of the Trinity

St Augustine is the great theologian who pursued the problem of the trinitarian image of God in the human soul. In the second half of *De Trinitate*, proceeding from the scriptural affirmation of genesis (1:26) that the human person is made in the image of God, Augustine looks to the human being for vestiges of the Trinity. Although in Book VIII, he touches upon the analogy of the lover, the beloved and the love itself, his preferred analogies are those derived from the human soul, the soul's memory, knowledge and love of itself, and more particularly, the soul's memory, knowledge and love of God. The difficulty with this approach is that the three persons in God are understood according to the analogy of the human soul closed in upon itself in its acts of knowing and willing.

In light of the consequences of this approach which I sketched above, a number of theologians today are urging us to seek a new path to discover *vestigia trinitatis* in the sphere of God's creation, namely the social image of God in human community. One important author to pursue this point is the American Jesuit theologian, Joseph Bracken. In a series of articles in the *Heythrop Journal* in 1974[12] and more recently in a larger study entitled *The Triune Symbol: Persons, Process and Community*, Bracken has pursued a rigorously communitarian model for understanding the Trinity. Early in this book Bracken states his central thesis: 'The nature or essence of God is to be an interpersonal process, i.e. a community of three divine persons who are constantly growing in knowledge and love of one another and who are thus themselves in process even as they constitute the divine community as a specifically social process.'[13]

Naturally, Bracken recognizes that his formulation is only acceptable if one thinks in new ontological categories. At least two presuppositions are essential here: first, that being itself is dynamic process; secondly, that to be is to be related.

Obviously a critical problem underlying Bracken's theory is the relationship between the individual and the community. If we think in substance categories, then each person is a substance in himself and the community is an aggregate of persons. If one is working with this ontology and speaks of the Trinity as a divine community, one will end up with a tritheistic conception. Bracken, however, does not accept these ontological assumptions. According to his ontology, the metaphysical reality of persons in community is higher than that of individual substance. For Bracken, a community represents an ontological unity which is greater than the sum of its parts. Rejecting the primacy of the Aristotelian category of substance, Bracken maintains that the unity of God is not the unity of substance but the unity of community. In the Trinity, community and person are strictly correlative. He writes, 'One and the same act of being therefore would constitute each of the three divine persons as an individual existent, and all of them together as a divine community.'[14]

According to this model, how would we understand the divine consciousness? We have already seen that the classical model and that pursued by Barth and Rahner hold for one act of divine consciousness. Bracken on the other hand maintains that there are three consciousnesses in the Trinity and indeed three freedoms but that there is a perfect harmony and correspondence between them. He notes, 'Even though each divine person has his own mind and will, they are of one mind and one will in everything they say and do, both with respect to one another and in their relationships with human beings and the whole of creation.'[15] Thus, whereas the classical tradition affirmed one consciousness proceeding from one simple and indivisible act of being, Bracken argues for a shared consciousness of three divine subjects.

The other contemporary thinker to pursue the same road as that of Bracken is Jürgen Moltmann. In numerous books and articles he vigorously pursues his social model of the Trinity.[16] Whereas Augustine took as his starting point the absolute indivisibility of the divine unity and proceeded from unity to triunity, Moltmann argues that we should do just the opposite and proceed from plurality to unity. On the basis of our experience of the three divine subjects in salvation history, we should proceed to the consideration of their unification in the divine life, a unification which Moltmann links closely to the unification of history in the eschatological Kingdom of God.

Rejecting like Bracken a philosophy of substance, Moltmann argues that being a person means being in relation. Moltmann thus considers the Trinity as the divine community of persons in relation. Here he picks up the classical concept of *perichoresis*. The being of the persons is their relationships. The persons of the Trinity are so intimately linked to one another that they mutually indwell one another. On the basis of this understanding of *perichoresis*, one can understand the Trinity as the divine *koinonia* rather than as the divine substance.

Many of Moltmann's colleagues have felt uneasy about his social doctrine of God, seeing in it a subtle form of tritheism. But he vigorously rejects the accusation, maintaining that it is based on a misconception of his metaphysical vision. According to Moltmann, a social vision of the Trinity would only be tritheistic if the persons were considered to exist in themselves and subsequently to enter into relations with one another. But Moltmann rules out this understanding of person as exclusively individualistic. The persons are their relationships and without the relationships there are no persons.

Finally it should be remarked that one of the strengths of Moltmann's approach is the impetus it gives to building human community. There has always been a close link between the *imago Dei* and the spiritual journey. Augustine said that a man should enter into himself, so that in his soul, he could begin the ascent to God. Because the Trinity is already implanted within the soul, the spiritual journey is possible, a journey which, according to Augustine, will only be complete in the soul's vision of God face-to-face. Moltmann's *imago trinitatis* leads to another spiritual journey. As he puts it, 'The Holy Trinity is our social programme.'[17] Because the human community is the *imago trinitatis*, men and women are summoned to correspond to the divine likeness. The Christian life, then, is a summons to community. And, just as for Augustine, so also for Moltmann, this summons is eschatological. The completion of the *imago trinitatis* will take place only in the eschaton when the Son will hand over the Kingdom to the Father. Then God will be all in all, and there will be one *koinonia*, all men and women united in the fellowship of the Father, the Son and the Holy Spirit.

The Search for a Synthesis

If we look at the history of the problem of 'person' in Christian theology, we see that there are at least two stages of development. There is first the classical stage which developed the metaphysical idea of person. Here the emphasis was on the distinctness of the three, and the objectivity of each person. This stage culminates in Aquinas's definition of the persons of the Trinity as distinct subsistent relations. The second stage of the development is what we might call the psychological one. Here the emphasis is on the person as a centre of consciousness and freedom. William Hill notes that there are three valuable points in the modern notion of person: consciousness of self and others, emphasis on relationality and focus upon intersubjectivity.[18]

Is there any way in which one can synthesize the classical, metaphysical approach and the contemporary psychological approach to the person? Here I would like to reappropriate a distinction which is certainly hinted at in Augustine and which is fully explicit in Aquinas and which is employed by a number of contemporary thinkers such as Hill, Bourassa, Lonergan and Kasper, namely the distinction between essential and personal acts in the Trinity.

Kasper argues that the doctrine of the Trinity is the Christian form of monotheism. The early church never thought of abandoning the monotheism of Judaism. God is one and his being is radically simple and indivisible. The unity of the Trinity is not one of number but one of being. Kasper points out that such radical simplicity excludes the possibility of three consciousnesses in God.

Nevertheless, as we saw above, Christian faith also wants to affirm that this radical unity is not incompatible with plurality. Hence there are three persons in God but each of the persons is identical with God himself. Each of the persons is God. In God essence and person are identical.

But can we now integrate the modern psychological understanding of person into trinitarian theology? Hill suggests that we can, but only in an analogical sense. According to Hill, one can say that there are distinct subjects of notional acts in the Trinity. For example, the Father alone begets the Son. The Son alone is the Father's Word. The Holy Spirit alone is the bond of communion between the Father and the Son. Hence we can speak of three subjects and of their reciprocity. And indeed we should speak of a *koinonia* but such language is analogous. For, in our human experience, although the subject is socially conditioned, his relationship to community always remains at the same time an act of free choice. His being in community is thus a task. Thus, whereas in human experience, person and community are not identical, in God they are. Nevertheless, respecting the analogical character of our language, I must agree with Hill when he writes:

> The persons in God thus constitute a divine intersubjectivity: Father, Son and Holy Spirit are three centres of consciousness in community, in mutual comunication. The members of the Trinity are now seen as constituting a community of persons in pure reciprocity, as subjects and centres of one divine conscious life. Each person is constituted by what might analogously be called an 'I' in self-awareness of its own unique identity, but only by way of rapport to the other two persons as a non-self; indeed, it is in virtue of that free interplay, wherein each person disposes himself towards the others in knowing and loving, that each person gains his unique identity.[19]

Let us return for a moment to the question of the divine consciousness. We said above that Kasper rules out three consciousnesses for God. But what I explained in the preceding paragraph would also exclude a monadic consciousness. Perhaps the best we can do is to say that the one divine consciousness is a shared consciousness, shared by the three persons. This is the position of Lonergan, one which is accepted by Hill, Bourassa and Kasper. Kasper writes, following Lonergan, 'We have no choice, then, but to say that in the Trinity we are dealing with three subjects who are reciprocally conscious of each other by reason of one and the same consciousness which the three subjects "possess" each in his own proper way.'[20]

To sum it up, we seem to be confronted here with an instance in theology where only a fine, but important distinction will enable us to clarify the problem and achieve some level of understanding. Here the appropriate distinction would be between essential and personal acts, between essential and personal consciousness. As to the consciousness of the three persons, Bourassa concludes with the following three points: (1) Each person is conscious of himself in the full plenitude of divinity (essential consciousness). (2) Each person is conscious of himself as distinct from the other persons (personal consciousness). (3) At the same time each person's consciousness of self is a total and reciprocal communication.

To put it in thesis form, I bring these reflections to a close with Bourassa's succinct summary formula, 'Consciousness in God is thus both an *essential* act of knowledge and love common to the three persons, and *personal* consciousness, exercised by each person, as consciousness of self, according to the personal action of each which is infinitely conscious and free, as pure and spontaneous love, in the most perfect reciprocity.'[21]

Analogy of Being and Analogy of Faith

The Problem of Vestigium Trinitatis

One of the perennial problems of Christian theology is whether and how human language can express the reality of God. If God is really transcendent and if our human language is radically limited to inner-worldly experience, it would seem that our language is incapable of bringing God into speech. At the same time the Christian experience of God is decisively shaped by God's revelation of himself in the humanity of Jesus of Nazareth. Thus it would seem that the Christian understanding of God requires that it be capable of being expressed in human language. The problem is all the more acute, when one is confronted with the theology of the Trinity. Kant, for example, was so convinced of the finitude of all our human concepts of God that he maintained that such a doctrine is incomprehensible, because it surpasses all our concepts.

One of the first great thinkers to wrestle with this problem was Augustine in his theory of the *vestigium trinitatis*. For Augustine, there were two non-negotiable truths: God is Trinity and the human being is made in the image of God (Gen. 1:26). On the basis of these two truths, he thought it was reasonable to look to the human mind for images or analogies of the divine life. In his *De Trinitate* Augustine offers a host of different analogies, but his preferred one is that of memory, intellect and will, i.e. the subject's self-presence which comes to thematic expression in self-knowledge and self-love. Aquinas appropriated this insight and worked out an elaborate metaphysical system to explore the inner-trinitarian life on the basis of the analogy of human intelligence and will.

Under the influence of Kantian agnosticism such attempts have been largely repudiated today. Besides philosophical motives, there have also been advanced strong theological reasons for the negation of this tradition. The principal spokesman for the opposition in our century has been Karl Barth. Let us examine some of his reflections on the problem of analogy.

Barth confronted this problem as early as the first volume of his great work *Church Dogmatics*. In an important section of the first volume which is dedicated to building the trinitarian scaffolding for all of Christian theology, Barth considers the problem of the Augustinian *vestigium trinitatis*. As is typical of Barth, he takes the problem seriously. The problem of the *vestigia* is not a peripheral one in theology. For it is in fact nothing less than the central question of language about God:

> It may be said that the problem involved was that of theological language, which can be none other than the language of the world and which, whatever the cost, must always speak and believes that it can speak, contrary to the natural capacity of this language, in this language, as theological language, of God's revelation. Regarded in this fundamental fashion, so far as it is susceptible of being so regarded – the doctrine of the *vestigia* was anything but playing with words![1]

Nonetheless, Barth vigorously rejects the doctrine of the *vestigia*. His reason is that he sees in this doctrine a dangerous tendency toward anthropocentrism. What is at stake here is nothing less than the uniqueness of revelation and the foundations of theological method. For Barth, human language has of itself no capacity to talk about God. We can and must talk about God only because God has revealed himself in his Word. God comes to speech in his Word of revelation. Theology's task is not to admit another source of revelation alongside of the Word of God. Rather, theology's task is to interpret this one and only Word which God addresses to humanity. Barth sees in the doctrine of the *vestigia* a dangerous tendency to admit another source for revelation alongside of God's Word. This source would be an anthropological one. On the basis of human experience as such, the human being thinks that he can say something about God. Barth vehemently rejects this idea. The fallacy in Augustine's doctrine is that he tries to illustrate revelation rather than interpret it.

Later in the *Church Dogmatics*, Barth developed these ideas more fully, repudiating any attempt to move from the human, from below, to God who is above. Thus he developed his well-known polemic against the Catholic doctrine of natural theology and its approach to theological language in the analogy of being. He called the doctrine of the analogy of being the anti-Christ and said that it was ultimately the decisive issue which divided Protestants and

Catholics and was the final reason why a Protestant could not become a Catholic.

Barth offers numerous reasons for his rejection of the Catholic doctrine of analogy. First, God and the world have nothing in common. God is so transcendent that we can in no way think of God and the world together. We cannot proceed from the world to God; we can only understand the world by proceeding from above to below. Analogy, on the contrary, tries to lump God and the world together under the concept of being. Secondly, Barth says that the doctrine of analogy is a product of human thinking and thus finite and relative. Third, he maintains that the doctrine can easily become a tool for our disobedience. Perhaps, most decisive of all, however, is Barth's conviction that the analogy of being can never reach the true God. The true God is the Father, the Son and the Holy Spirit, the God who becomes accessible to us in Jesus Christ. The analogy of being does not lead us to this God but only to an abstraction. It leads us perhaps, as the First Vatican Council affirmed, to the principle and end of all things. But it does not lead us to the God who is Lord, Creator, Redeemer and Reconciler.

What should we say in the face of this serious assault on the classical doctrine of analogy? First, I think that we can admit that there is at least an element of truth in this critique, especially if we look at the question historically, from the viewpoint of Catholic theology since Vatican I. The danger of Catholic theology in the period between the two Vatican Councils was that it was dualistic. It constructed its theory of the knowability of God according to the two-storey conception of nature and supernature. One was easily given the impression that the theologian first began by constructing a philosophical account of God, his existence and his attributes and then on top of this a properly theological account of the Trinity on the basis of supernatural revelation. Barth's rejection of this scheme is justified. Such a philosophical account of God is indeed an abstraction. Today, however, Catholic theology has firmly rejected such dualism. For this reason, we began our reflection upon God in this book with the fact of God's revelation of himself. The best of Catholic theology today argues that the philosophical moment is a moment within the theological moment itself, not a propaedeutic to it. To be fair, however, if one looks back to the riches of the patristic period and in particular to the theology of

Augustine, one notices that Augustine is not a dualist. His reflections on the *vestigium trinitatis* occur only in the second half of his great work. Only after having firmly rooted the trinitarian faith in the scriptures and in the church's teaching, does Augustine begin the second theological *démarche*, the speculative effort to understand. Thus, within faith and on the basis of faith's conviction that the human person is made in God's image, Augustine looks to the human mind for a key to open the mystery of the divine life.

If Barth's critique has its moment of truth, we must also say that it contains a serious distortion, for Barth so dichotomizes the God-world relation that God can no longer be found in the world, nor can the world correspond to him. Thus ironically Barth himself falls into a type of dualism. Hans Urs von Balthasar criticizes Barth along these lines when he points out that Barth's conception does not take the human being seriously as God's covenant partner.[2] Although Barth appropriates the covenant theme as a central motif in his theological vision, he so exaggerates the one-way character of God's revelation to the world, that the human person is deprived of his freedom and the world is robbed of its autonomous structures, so that God ends up in a dialogue with himself. If there is to be a genuine dialogical situation, Balthasar argues that the structures of creation must be preserved within the order of redemption and grace.

While never retracting his rejection of the analogy of being, Barth's christological starting point led him ever more in the direction of analogy. One could see the progression of Barth's theological opus as the gradual move away from dialectic toward analogy. This was inevitable once Barth came to see that Jesus Christ is the Lord of creation. Because of Christ's sovereign Lordship Barth perceived ever more clearly that the creation was good and that its structures could never be destroyed. Barth's own way of conceiving the two orders of creation and redemption was in terms of covenant. For Barth, the external ground of the covenant is the creation. The internal ground of the covenant is Jesus Christ. The creation exists for the sake of Christ and Christ preserves it integrally in its goodness. Balthasar therefore argues that there should be no contradiction between the analogy of being and the analogy of faith. The analogy of being, rooted in the creation, exists within the analogy of faith. A christocentrism such as Barth's need not be inimical to the best insights of the classical Catholic tradition. In this sense, Balthasar argues for a christologically founded analogy of being. Let us explain this idea at greater length. How can we understand the analogy of being and the analogy of faith in such a way that they are not contradictory but complementary? Perhaps as a heuristic clue, we could take two principles which at first seem to be contradictory but which I would argue need to be held in constant tension. The first is that of the Fourth Lateran Council: for all the similarity between God and the world, the similarity is embraced within an even greater dissimilarity. This principle points to the God who is ever greater, to the transcendence of God. The other principle is based on God's staggering condescension to us in the kenosis of the Incarnation and the cross: for all the dissimilarity between God and humanity, the dissimilarity is embraced within an even greater similarity. Let us look at each principle in turn, beginning with the first principle, which sums up the classical analogy of being, and which aims at preserving God's transcendence and points to the divine as the ever-abiding Mystery.

Analogy of Being: Aquinas

There is no better representative of the classical Catholic position on analogy than Thomas Aquinas. One of Aquinas's great achievements was to appropriate and deepen the Augustinian tradition with its neo-Platonic structures and to integrate into this vision the insights of Aristotle which were being discovered anew in the thirteenth century.

According to one well-known commentator on St Thomas, Fr Norris Clarke,[3] it is important to bear in mind Aquinas's neo-Platonic participation-metaphysics. The clue to the Thomistic synthesis is the participation of all created reality in God the Creator. Aquinas took over the formal structure of neo-Platonic participation theory, emptied it of its excessive Platonic realism of ideas and filled it with the new wine of his own quite original insight into the act of existence as the ultimate positive core of all real perfections. Plato had sought the unity of reality in the realm of ideas. Aquinas transposes the search for unity to the level of existence. Combining this insight with the Aristotelian framework, Aquinas can think of all finite reality as composed of two metaphysical principles, act and potency. But then Aquinas draws the multiple finite acts of existence (limited by potency) back to their ultimate source in God, who is *Ipsum Esse Subsistens*. The core of Aquinas's metaphysical argument for God's existence is that diversity as such can never be the ultimate explanation of unity. But where there is a real perfection shared by many (in this case the act of existence), it must be possible to seek the source of similarity in a single common origin. As Clarke puts it, 'Since existence itself is the most universally shared of all perfections, including all that is real in any way, there must be a single common ultimate Source of all existence from whence all others participate in it, each in its own way.'[4] Implicit in this argumentation are two other principles which Aquinas more or less takes for granted: first, the principle of causality as a heuristic principle governing the search for the intelligibility of things and secondly the conviction that what is caused must be similar to that which causes it.

These two principles lead us to the doctrine of analogy and to the possibility of using human language, based on human experience of the finite world, to speak of the transcendent source of that reality. First, let us pause for a moment to reflect on how analogy actually functions in the human process of discovery. Clarke argues that the human mind is always on the search for intelligibility and unity and seeks to catch the similarities and affinities running up and down and across the universe. Analogy is thus in his terms a stretch-concept by which the mind seeks to proceed from the known to the unknown. Human intelligence in its drive to know seeks to establish on the basis of what it already knows a beach-head in a new and as yet unexplored level of reality or being. As an example of this heuristic process, Clarke mentions how Freud found it necessary to postulate the existence of a subconscious and unconscious dimension of cognitive activity in the human person and thus extended the term 'cognition' to embrace a new level of reality, the unconscious. On the basis of the effects of manifesting themselves in conscious experience, he postulated a source of these effects in the unconscious. The meaning of the cognitive was extended to embrace a new level of reality.

How does this type of heuristic approach work with regard to religious language? Before answering this question, it would be helpful to refer to another distinction in the classical theory of analogy, namely the distinction between the analogy of proportionality and the analogy of attribution. The analogy of proportionality is based on four terms such that a:b :: c:d. But this type of analogy presupposes that all four terms are known. An example would be: evening is to day as old age is to life. In this simple analogy, one proceeds from a well-known experience of everyday to illumine a quality of human life. Such an analogy is problematic as regards religious language, because language is transcendent, and therefore beyond this world and our finite experience. Consequently we know only one side of the proportion. To overcome this difficulty, a second type of analogy is discussed, that of attribution. Here we have several realities which are similar to a third thing. The third thing is the prime analogate in terms of which the others are seen to be similar. A type of food or physical exercise can be said to be healthy because we know what health is in the human person.

It is commonly said that Aquinas combines these two types of analogy. He can draw proportions between the divine reality and the created reality, because the basis of these analogies of proportionality is the analogy of attribution. The analogy of attribution in turn makes sense within the context of Aquinas's participation-metaphysics. Because all finite being participates in God as the Ultimate Source of existence and because there is a similarity between cause and effect, it must be possible to predicate finite perfections of God once they have been purified of their finite limitations. This is the origin of the classical three-fold way of ascent to God, the *via negativa*, the *via positiva* and the *via emenentiae*. However, when one sees that according to Aquinas, the ultimate source of unity is existence itself, one grasps as well that the only language adequate to speak of God is the language of the transcendental properties of being, i.e. those qualities which belong to any being insofar as it is. Classically, these attributes are unity, truth, beauty and goodness. God, as the source of all being, is one, true, beautiful and good and the source of all these perfections in creatures who possess them in limited degrees. Hence all language about God is perforce analogical. We can say, for example, that God is beautiful. But such a statement is analogous because positively we know what beauty is only in our human finite experience. On the basis of causality, however, we know that God must be the ultimate source of beauty. Still, such an affirmation is shrouded in darkness, for we cannot say positively what beauty is like in itself, in the infinite, transcendent God. Analogical language about God is elusive, for in the very moment in which we must speak about God, God slips beyond our grasp. Grasping him, we must let him go. Clarke speaks of analogy as the language of *chiaroscuro*, a mixture of light and darkness. He also explains that analogical language is vector-like; it is directional language. It points us to God, but without ever being able to grasp him in concepts. Analogical language is the language of revelation and concealment, which points us to the ultimate Mystery, the God ever greater. In this sense, Barth was wrong when he rejected the analogy of being as a threat to God's transcendence and as the occasion of sin for human pride and disobedience. The logic of analogy leads the human person to surrender before the unfathomable Mystery which can never be controlled. Analogy precisely lets God be God. In the language of the Fourth Lateran Council, for all the similarity between the creature and the Creator, the similarity is embraced within an ever greater dissimilarity. Nonetheless, we must ask ourselves whether the analogy of being is the final truth about the human capacity to speak about God. For if this transcendent God has drawn near to us in Christ, if he has revealed himself in a human being, if he has come to speak in a human life, must we not be able to say more? This leads us once again to the analogy of faith.

Analogy of Faith: the Crucified

Karl Rahner, in developing his theological anthropology, argues that the human person is a hearer of the Word. As a creature, the human being is so ordered to Mystery that he listens either to the silence of God or to a word which the Mystery speaks to him. Coming from the evangelical tradition, Eberhard Jüngel argues that the most basic structure of the human being is revealed in dialogue. The person comes to himself because he is addressed. His being spoken to leads him to question. For both theologians, it is of decisive significance for the life of faith that God breaks his silence and addresses human beings, summoning them to be his covenant partners.

Let us follow Jüngel and say that the decisive moment where this revelation occurs is the death and resurrection of Jesus.[5] In the paschal mystery, we see the event of revelation *par excellence*. God, who is beyond the world, identifies himself with this man Jesus, dead upon the cross. The implications of this identification are profound. First, we are challenged to think of God in union with the world. Secondly, we are led to think the eternal God in union with an historical event, in union with the temporal and perishable. Thirdly, we see here the union of life and death in such a way that God declares himself in favour of life rather than death. The paschal mystery is the triumph of life over the destructiveness of death.

We should also mention two other implications of this identification of God with Jesus on the cross. First, if God is the radically transcendent one, beyond the world and temporality, and if God identifies himself with the historical, then this implies a movement in God. God comes to the world in Jesus Christ. But God not only comes to the world, he also draws near in such a way that he comes to speech. Here Jüngel builds on the theology of revelation of the school of Ebeling and Fuchs, who speak of God's revelation as a language-event. If God has identified himself with Jesus, then the whole life of Jesus, including his proclamation of the Kingdom, is revealed as God's Word to the world. But even more important, since God identifies himself with the dead Jesus, raising him to life, thus achieving the victory of life over death, the Word which Jesus preached is transformed into the Word of the kerygma. The resurrection gives rise to the preaching of the community. There follows inevitably the transition from the word of Jesus about the Kingdom to Jesus as the Word of God in whom God continues to come to expression.

Can we be more precise about how this language-event is to be understood? Jüngel argues that the key is analogy. However, at this point we see the difference (not the contradiction) between the analogy of being and the analogy of faith. The neuralgic point of all religious language is anthropomorphism.[6] But as we have seen, the analogy of being has the function to point us to the God who is beyond the world and thus the analogy of being shows how religious language can be purified of its anthropomorphism to point us in the direction of that which cannot be said. The analogy of faith, on the other hand, is oriented to let God come into language. The analogy of faith unashamedly accepts the necessity of a certain anthropomorphism. As Jüngel puts it, this analogy does not speak of God like a man but speaks of God as a man. In this analogy of faith, rooted in the paschal mystery, there is an identification of God and the human.

If we look back over the types of analogy we sketched above, we recall that in the analogy of proportionality, the proportion was as follows a:b :: c:d. We saw that this schema as such was inadequate for religious language, because God remained an unknown x. In the schema which Jüngel suggests, God comes to the world in his revelation in such a way that x is no longer unknown. Jüngel diagrams the relationship this way: x:a :: b:c. God comes to the world in such a way that worldly reality corresponds to him. An illustration of this in the life of Jesus would be his use of parables. Jesus begins his parables, 'The Kingdom of God is like . . .'. The extraordinary situations which Jesus describes in his parables, such as the man who sells all that he has to buy a field in which a treasure is hidden, do not of themselves contain the possibility of speaking of God. But they are co-opted by Jesus and so integrated into his situation as prophet of the Kingdom, that God's Kingdom becomes an event which comes into language through them. God so uses human language that it corresponds to him.

In one of his essays entitled 'Metaphorical Truth' Jüngel draws on Heidegger's understanding of truth to enrich this interpretation of religious language. Heidegger's background as a Catholic led him to link the ideas of revelation and truth. As a Catholic, Heidegger had learnt that revelation was an unveiling. His study of Greek philosophy prompted him to explore the idea of truth as *aletheia*. Philosophically this led Heidegger to say that truth is an event in which Being unveils itself. Being so addresses man that it lets itself be discovered. Jüngel appropriates these ideas for his theology of revelation. He stresses the event character of revelation and of truth. God becomes unveiled in the event of the cross. At the same time Jüngel stresses the relationship between event and language. The event of revelation is an unveiling which comes to speech in the kerygma. Speech about God is not a subsequent moment of that revelation. The revelation-event and the speech-event are two sides of one reality. As Jüngel puts it, 'In speech God lets himself be discovered as the one who comes.'[7]

Jüngel's understanding of the analogy of faith adds an important new dimension which the analogy of being was unable to express. According to the analogy of being, we human beings know that we are referred to God, but we do not know if God is referred to us. According to the analogy of being the human person is made for Mystery, but Mystery slips beyond his grasp into silence. The analogy of faith, however, is rooted in the fact that God speaks and addresses us. God wants to be for us and to place himself in relation to us. God's identification of himself with the cross of Jesus, which comes to expression in the kerygma, enables us to formulate the being of God as love. The philosophical doctrine of analogy only enables us to say what God is not. The theological doctrine of analogy enables us to say what God is. The analogy of faith enables us to do justice to the biblical affirmation that God is love (1 John 4:16). In this sense, the analogy of faith requires us to express the condescension of God and his incredible nearness: for all the dissimilarity between God and the world, the dissimilarity is embraced within an even greater similarity.

The Story of Jesus as the Parable of God

If we hearken back to the beginning of this chapter and the critique which Karl Barth made of Augustine's doctrine of the *vestigium trinitatis*, we will recall that Barth feared a second source of revelation which would lead to an anthropocentric theology. Nevertheless Barth saw clearly that Christian faith cannot by-pass the human. God comes to us as a human being. Thinking along these lines, he entitled one of his late works *The Humanity of God*. But even as early as the first volume of *Church Dogmatics*, he did not hesitate to say that Jesus is the genuine *vestigium trinitatis*. Let us explore this notion at greater depth, by appropriating a more contemporary expression: the story of Jesus as the parable of God.

One of the significant areas of biblical research in recent years has been the parables of Jesus. Concomitant with this study, there has been a renewed investigation of the parable as a literary form. Since the time of the Enlightenment, philosophical reflection has made us more aware that it is too simplistic merely to think of reality as something objective 'out there'. All reality is in fact reality for a subject. It is too facile to think that the world presents itself as *facta bruta* for objective presentation. Rather, reality is constantly being interpreted by the subject. An example of this can be found in the visual arts. When Picasso painted a human face, he was not merely representing an external reality. He was painting what he saw. The test of his genius is whether through his art he can reconstruct the viewer's perception so that the viewer now sees the way Picasso sees. Through the work of art the perceiver is able to behold what previously he was unable to see.[8] In this context the biblical scholar, John Dominic Crossan affirms that the most appropriate way to come to terms with reality is to tell stories.[9] Apart from the stories we tell we have no access to reality. We live in the midst of story.

Crossan points out that two fundamental types of story are myth and parable. Myth is a story which has the function of reconciling contradictories. Parable, on the other hand, has the function of creating irreconciliation. Parable is by its very nature subversive. It has a shock effect which challenges our accepted conventions of meaning. Crossan writes, 'The function of parable is to create contradiction within a given situation of complacent security, but even more unnervingly, to challenge the fundamental principle of reconciliation by making us aware of the fact that we made up the reconciliation.'[10]

Another aspect of parable which Crossan stresses is its event character. Like a joke, the parable is an event. It has to succeed. Parable is meant to provoke a reaction within the listener which either succeeds or fails to achieve its goal. When Nathan the prophet tells King David the parable of the ewe lamb, David is provoked to righteous indignation (2 Sam. 12). But all his pre-established ideas are shattered when the prophet declares: 'You are that man.' In that moment David sees reality differently. The parable succeeds and David repents.

These ideas help us to understand better how God comes into language. We noted above how the Kingdom of God comes into speech through Jesus's parables. We also noted that the supreme moment of revelation is the event in which God identifies himself with the cross and resurrection of Jesus. It is important to stress that this act of revelation is an event, something which happens in history. But like other events it is graspable only through language. The event must be narrated, it is a story to be told. Moreover, it fits the literary genre of parable. As a number of commentators have suggested, it is through the paschal mystery that Jesus, the parabler, becomes the parable of God.[11] Why?

The answer is that here, if anywhere, we have an event which subverts all our ideas about God. We do not encounter Jesus without any previous notion of God. Nor did Jesus's Jewish contemporaries. The Pharisees expected a God who would stand on the side of the morally righteous person, who would come to the defence of the just and would reward the pious. Jesus in his life challenged such an understanding. By his identification with tax-collectors and sinners, Jesus preached a God who stood on the side of the irreligious and the God-forsaken, a God of mercy rather than revenge. Jesus entrusted his whole life to such a God who would vindicate himself by bringing about his reign. In our expectations of God, we often project a concept of God derived from what we would like to be – all-powerful, invulnerable, unaffected by suffering and hurt. On the cross all these expectations are shattered. God does not come to the rescue of Jesus. Jesus who stood in solidarity with the God-forsaken becomes himself the God-forsaken. As Moltmann says, the cross is either the end of all theology or the beginning of a specifically Christian theology. Because faith (through the event of the resurrection) perceives the cross of Christ as God's identification with human God-forsakenness, we are shaken out of our complacency in parabolic fashion and are challenged to think God anew. God is all-powerful because he can make himself weak. God is high because he can bend down and make himself low. God's greatness consists in his vulnerability to human suffering and misery. In short, God is love. Such a statement is not a philosophical statement. It is a statement which is based on an event in which God gives himself to speech.

Crossan says that parables give room to God. They give a space in which God can be God. They allow God to be a God of surprises. Certainly the cross of Christ can be said to be a parable in this sense. Crossan also makes the point that a parable allows that to which it points to become visible. Again this is verified in the death of Jesus. Understood as a parable of God, this event allows God's love to become visible for the world. Finally, Crossan argues that a parable never becomes dispensable. It is never like the first stage of a rocket which is aborted once the space-craft is launched. A parable remains indispensable as the vehicle for the revelation of truth. It is not an illustration of a general principle but rather it is the means through which truth becomes an event. If this is the case, then Barth's fear about the *vestigium trinitatis* is obviated. For Barth, human language about God must never try to illustrate revelation but must interpret it. Human language, according to Barth, cannot illustrate revelation, for it lacks this capacity and therefore human language of its own capacity cannot say who God is. Our language, however, can interpret revelation, for revelation is the event which expresses itself in speech. When God's revelation in Christ happens, it becomes an event, which expresses itself in the parable of the life of Jesus, thus making room for God in human history.

Analogy as Correspondence

Our discussion thus far has been oriented to the christological dimension of analogy and the relation between the orders of creation and redemption. However, we should not forget that another dimension is also involved, which is of utmost spiritual significance for the human being, the dimension of grace. If up to this point we have focused on the analogy of being and on God's advent in the analogy of faith, we can here recapture the significance of the analogy of proportionality. This type of analogy is especially important for Hans Urs von Balthasar, who draws from it significant consequences for the spiritual life.[12]

Balthasar's dialogue partners are Karl Barth and Erich Przywara. Balthasar is convinced of the necessity of a theology of covenant, as Barth proposed it. His critique of Barth is, as we have seen, that Barth does not develop adequately a theological anthropology which does justice to human freedom. With regard to the philosophy of Przywara, Balthasar respects his appropriation of the Fourth Lateran Council's principle of the ever greater dissimilarity between God and the creation. He also sympathizes with Przywara's identification with the Dionysian tradition of theology. The human soul is on an upward ascent toward the unfathomable Mystery. Balthasar's critique is that Przywara so stresses the aspect of altereity that he neglects the dimension of correspondence. The soul is not only a restless striving toward God. Rather each human person is invited to share in the divine life according to his or her unique mission. Hence there is also the element of rest on the spiritual journey.

Let us unfold this vision in greater detail by commenting briefly on three key terms in the spirituality of Balthasar: exchange, surrender and correspondence. First of all, Balthasar's vision is firmly rooted in the patristic notion of the *admirable commercium*. God has become what we are in order that we might become what he is. The goal of God's self-communication is our divinization, i.e. our participation in the revelation-event and our sharing in the divine life.

Secondly, the key to this divinization is obedience. This is verified first of all in the life of Jesus himself. In Jesus we see a perfect identity between his Sonship and his mission. He is the Son by being the perfect receptivity to the Father's offer of love and to the Father's desire to save. His human life is a working out of this inner-trinitarian obedience. In the same way, each human being is called upon by God to share in Christ's mission in some unique way which is known to God alone. Every man or woman has a unique sending in this world and the only way to realize one's identity is to surrender to this call.

Finally, by such a surrender in obedience, a person corresponds to God. If Christ is the perfect parable of the Father, or as Balthasar would put it, the analogy of being in person, then each human person is called to share in that analogy and thus create in his or her life an analogy of proportionality. When this happens, the *imago trinitatis* takes shape within the life of the human person. The *vestigium trinitatis* then is not only found in Jesus Christ but is realized anew in each human being. In this perspective, we can see that the problem of analogy is not only a theoretical one, limited to ontological and epistemological concerns, but touches as well the foundations of the life of grace and our participation in the divine Mystery.

Analogy and Eschatology

In his discussion of metaphor, Jüngel points out that metaphor has the function of widening the horizon of being to discover something new. Analogical language, we have seen, is not only descriptive of what is, but makes room for the God who comes. In this perspective it is useful to recall that we should not think of analogy in a static way but should integrate the doctrine of analogy into a dynamic perspective. In *The God of Jesus Christ*, Walter Kasper makes a suggestion along these lines when he says that our contemporary awareness of our historicity should prompt us to re-think the doctrine of analogy on the basis of freedom.[13] In every human act, the human subject is driven beyond himself toward the infinite. With-

out this infinite horizon within which he acts, he could never be free
vis-à-vis finite objects. The distance between the finite and the
infinite is the condition which makes finite freedom possible. At the
same time, this implicit awareness of the infinite can only become
concrete in the world and in history. As Kasper puts it, analogy:

> ... leads us to see the world anew within the horizon of freedom
> and to understand the world as the place where freedom is
> exercised ... The doctrine of analogy, when thus transformed,
> can therefore disclose to us the possibilities present in reality;
> this means, it can disclose reality's dimension of futurity. The
> pre-apprehension characteristic of freedom is thus an anticipa-
> tion of a future that is more than an extrapolated past and
> present.[14]

In this book I have often emphasized that our knowledge of God
is rooted in the paschal mystery. For the Lutheran tradition such
knowledge implies that God's true being is revealed under the form
of his contrary. A modern commentator such as Moltmann has thus
advocated a dialectical method for coming to know God. Nonetheless even Moltmann sees the necessity of analogy, precisely to
preserve Christianity's eschatological vision. As Moltmann notes,
dialectic cannot replace analogy but rather makes it possible for the
first time; that is, God's action in Christ, especially on the cross,
makes possible the human correspondence to God which we spoke
of above. As he writes, 'Insofar as God is revealed in his opposite,
he can be known by the godless and those who are abandoned by
God, and it is this knowledge which brings them into correspondence with God and, as 1 John 3:2 says, enables them to have the
hope of being like God.'[15] Thus God's being revealed as love in the
paschal mystery opens up the future of the world which has as its
goal the new creation in Christ. As St John says in the text referred
to by Moltmann, 'We are God's children now; it does not yet appear
what we shall be, but we know that when he appears we shall be like
him, for we shall see him as he is.'

VIII

Trinitarian Faith and Praxis

Introduction

As the *leitmotiv* for this chapter, we could take the famous objection of Immanuel Kant who wrote, 'From the doctrine of the Trinity taken literally, nothing whatsoever can be gained for practical purposes, even if one believed that one comprehended it – and still less if one is conscious that it surpasses all our concepts.'[1] Kant presupposes that the trinitarian faith of the church is a pure theory which has no practical relevance for life.

The type of divorce between theory and praxis of which Kant accuses Christian theology is not only serious in itself but is all the more grave in the light of the radical challenge issued by Karl Marx who showed that there is no such thing as a neutral theory. According to Marx, theories always arise out of praxis and feed back into it. Marx refuted the idealistic approach to theory and action, according to which the philosopher creates a system of thought and subsequently applies it to a concrete situation. Marx showed that the relation between theory and action is dialectical. As Matthew Lamb explains, praxis grounds theory.[2] But praxis is not unreflective action. For Marx, praxis is action infused with and made conscious of itself by theory. Praxis is human activity that has the power to transform reality and make it more human. If praxis is the foundation of theory, it is also the goal of theory. Thus praxis and theory are related dialectically – praxis acts as a corrective of theory and theory modified by praxis transforms the given situation. This dialectical relation between theory and praxis is on-going.

If we apply these insights to the Christian doctrine of God, we can say that this doctrine or theory arises out of a concrete praxis. The Christian understanding of God has not fallen from heaven. As we have seen, it has arisen from our concrete experience of God in Jesus Christ, especially in his paschal mystery. This knowledge becomes concrete for us in the praxis of discipleship. As we relive what Jesus did and follow him, especially in his paschal mystery, we know the God who was revealed in these events to be Father, Son and Holy Spirit. In this perspective, taking account of the priority of praxis over theory, J. B. Metz writes, 'The salvation that is founded "for all men" in Christ does not become universal via an idea, but via the intelligible power of a praxis, the praxis of following Christ.'[3] Consistent with this viewpoint, Metz stresses that two of the fundamental categories of Christian theology are memory and narrative. According to idealistic interpretations of reality, the real is the rational and vice versa. Reality can be grasped by reason alone. But Christianity as an historical faith has never believed this. Christianity is bound to a free, gratuitous, unpredictable revelation of God in Jesus Christ and in his cross. The Christian doctrine of God is thus always bound to the story of Jesus. This fact indicates that memory will also be a central category of Christian thinking. The Christian vision of God is rooted in its memory of Jesus, of what he proclaimed and lived, and especially of his death and resurrection. But again, as Metz stresses, this memory is not detached from reality. He dares to call it a dangerous memory, for it remembers how God intervened in human affairs on the side of the poor, the rejected and the God-forsaken. Since God gave the victory to the crucified Christ, remembering him threatens all present structures of oppression, by summoning the poor, the rejected and the God-forsaken, to hope in the new future which the scripture calls God's Kingdom. In this sense the fundamental hope of the Bible can rightly be called liberation and its vision can even be called revolutionary. God is not on the side of the *status quo*. As St Paul says, 'the old has passed away, behold the new has come (2 Cor. 5:17)'. Let us then try to develop in greater detail the relationship between Christian praxis and the Christian understanding of God, beginning as Metz suggests, with the story of Jesus.

Jesus as the Justice of God

In an article relating Jesus to justice, John Haughey notes that many Christians today need to re-image Jesus in terms of justice.[4] In order to do this, it is first of all important to situate our understanding of the story of Jesus within the Old Testament understanding of God as the God of justice. To comprehend the Old Testament idea of God, it is also critical not to import into theology a narrow understanding of justice according to which justice is the minimum which a person is due nor to link the idea of justice to vindictiveness and punishment. At least two central ideas are critical for the Old Testament understanding of the God of justice. First, God is the

God who acts on behalf of his people. God liberates and frees his people from slavery in their exodus from Egypt. Secondly, God enters into a covenantal relationship, binding himself to Israel. John Donahue points out that, for the Old Testament, justice can be described as fidelity to the demands of a relationship.[5] God manifests his justice by being faithful to his covenant. A number of authors explain that, for the Old Testament, justice is such a comprehensive term that it is equivalent to the salvation which God offers and effects for his people. Thus the people of the Old Testament can pray without fear that God work his justice (Ps. 82:3-4), for this means that God will vindicate his people. God's justice, then, is his saving justice which has a special regard for the afflicted. God manifests his fidelity to his covenant by looking to those persons and groups within Israel most in danger of being exploited: the poor, the widow, the orphan, the sojourner. Thus there is no contradiction between God's justice and mercy, nor between the God of justice and the God of salvation. In fact they are equivalent. As José Míguez Bonino expresses it:

> God acts in righteousness when he establishes and re-establishes right relationships, restoring those who have been wronged in their legitimate claims as members of the covenant. Such action is the equivalent of 'salvation'. When God liberates Israel, when he protects the unprotected, when he delivers the captive or vindicates the right of the poor, he is exhibiting his justice.[6]

When Jesus began his mission, he associated his ministry with proclaiming and making present in sign and deed the Kingdom of God. This Kingdom which Jesus announced was precisely a Kingdom of justice, that is, a new order in which the human condition broken by sin, would be restored. Humankind's relationship to God and relationships between human persons on this earth would be as God intended them. God would create a new righteousness and was in fact already doing so.

The evangelists frequently associate the ministry of Jesus with God's justice. We have already seen (in Chapter 3) how St Luke links Jesus with Isaiah 61. In his inaugural sermon, Jesus proclaims, 'The Spirit of the Lord is upon me ... to set at liberty those who are oppressed, to proclaim the acceptable year of the Lord.' (Lk.

4:18–19). St Matthew associates Jesus with the servant of Isaiah 42, 'Behold my servant whom I have chosen ... I will put my Spirit upon him and he shall proclaim justice to the nations ... He will not break a bruised reed, or quench a smoldering wick, till he brings justice to victory.' (Mt. 12:17–21).

Jesus embodied this role in his ministry by identifying with the poor. According to the beatitudes, they are the ones who are in a position to understand his gospel. He castigates the Pharisees for their hypocrisy, since they use religion to exploit the oppressed. Unless the righteousness of his disciples exceeds that of the Pharisees, they shall not enter the Kingdom of God. He associates with tax-collectors and sinners and other fringe groups such as zealots, for they are the ones in need of God's mercy. As John Donahue points out, in this choice of ministry on the part of our Lord, we see that justice and mercy are not opposed but are in paradoxical agreement. And Bonino argues that we could sum up the early mission of Jesus in terms of justice, 'Jesus's mission is to proclaim and to be the "true king" of prophetic expectation, whose authority is exercised according to God's will, who cares for the poor, who offers himself for his people, who announces and inaugurates the "year of God's liberation".'[7] But since Jesus not only proclaims God's Kingdom of justice but also lives it in sign and deed, such as his table-fellowship with sinners, we can say that he is the incarnation of God's justice or righteousness. In his life the new order of being which God wills is coming to visible expression. Jesus incarnated in a paradigmatic way God's just and liberating rule.

But we must go on to note that the supreme paradigm of God's saving justice is the paschal mystery itself. First of all, as Moltmann has reminded us, we cannot think of Jesus's death apart from its historical situation. Jesus's death was no accident. His identification with tax-collectors led to his rejection by the Jewish authorities as a blasphemer. His association with zealots led to his execution as a political criminal. His was not the death of a martyr but the ignominious death of one killed outside the sacred walls (Heb. 13:13). Finally his identification with sinners was so complete that he took on the condition of God-forsakenness, dying with the loud cry, 'My God, my God, why hast Thou forsaken me?' (Mk. 15:34).

In the death of Jesus, we reach a decisive and unavoidable question both for the doctrine of God and for human hope. If Jesus merely perished on the cross, if his story is merely another tragedy of one who lived for an unattainable ideal, an ideal broken by the destructive forces of history, then gone is the hope of the kingdom of righteousness, of the totally new reality which Jesus preached. In this sense the death of Jesus implies a crisis of human hope. But, as Moltmann argues, it is also a crisis of God. Either God is dead or God has identified himself with the crucified Christ. For us believers, whose faith is founded on the resurrection, only the latter is a real option. The resurrection of the crucified Christ inspires a transformation of our understanding of God. For if Jesus is raised, then God did not abandon him. Rather God was on his side and took his part. But this implies an even more radical understanding of the God of the covenant. Here in the cross, we see the depths of what it means that God identifies himself with the poor, the outcast, the rejected, the God-forsaken. But if God has identified himself with the poor and rejected Christ, this identification has radical implications for our praxis of discipleship. It is to these implications that we must now turn.

Living Between the Times

The resurrection of Jesus is the overcoming of the apparent defeat of the cross. But it is more. It is also the confirmation of his mission and identity. Jesus is confirmed as God's righteousness incarnate. But if Jesus during his life-time anticipated the Kingdom of God, then his resurrection is the sure hope that God has destined us for the new creation. It is for this reason that the first Christians had such an intense longing for the parousia. They cried out, 'Come, Lord Jesus', for the resurrection of Jesus made them feel more keenly their present state of alienation, suffering and death. Jesus's resurrection, then, first of all points us away from our present state of affairs to God's eschatological Kingdom. But does this longing for the new creation not reveal that Marx's criticism of religion is true, namely that it is opium for the people to deaden their pain? Does it not turn us away from this world and render us passive in the face of the massive suffering which takes place on our earth?

One must accept Marx's indictment of Christianity to the extent that it is true that Christians believe that no human effort can bring about the Kingdom. Nor can God's Kingdom be associated with any inner-worldly utopia. In this sense Rahner does not hesitate to call

Christianity realistic pessimism. On the other hand, theologians such as Metz have pointed out, that Christianity offers a healthy antidote to evolutionary world-views based on the dubious idea of progress. Christianity with its hope of a radically new creation takes into account not only the hopes of present victims but also the victims of the past and the wastage of evolution. In the Christian vision, with its hope for the resurrection of the dead, there is hope that all the suffering of past generations can be redeemed. Metz speaks of Christianity's backward solidarity with the dead.[8]

But what of the charge that Christianity leads to an attitude of passivity? What is at stake here is how one conceives the relation between the Kingdom of God and present experience. In other words, what is the relation between history and eschatology?

In general I think one must say that there are both continuities and discontinuities between the Kingdom of God (the new creation) and present history. There is discontinuity because the Kingdom of God transcends history and no human effort can bring it about. But there are also continuities. *Gaudium et Spes* hinted at this truth in the words, 'While earthly progress must be carefully distinguished from the growth of Christ's Kingdom, to the extent that the former can contribute to the better ordering of human society, it is of vital concern to the Kingdom of God.' (no. 39, 1). Speaking along the same lines, the *Instruction on Christian Freedom and Liberation* in its comments on the relationship between eschatological hope and commitment to temporal liberation, affirmed that 'this distinction is not a separation; for man's vocation to eternal life does not suppress but confirms his task of using the energies and means which he has received from the creator for developing his temporal life.'[9]

We might ask at this point whether it is possible to make this line of thought more specific. Here I find the scheme proposed by Jürgen Moltmann helpful. Moltmann, reviewing some attempts, especially within the Protestant tradition, to understand the relationship between the earthly and the heavenly cities, suggests as a model what he calls eschatological christology.[10] First of all, because Christ is risen, the Spirit has been poured out on the world. Under the power of the Spirit men and women carry on Jesus's work of announcing and making present the Kingdom of God in signs and deeds. The Spirit leads human beings to create anticipations of the coming Kingdom. In Moltmann's words, 'These anticipations are not yet the Kingdom of God itself. But they are real mediations of the Kingdom of God within the limited possibilities of history.'[11] The other action of the Spirit is to create forces of resistance against all those manifestations of death which destroy human beings. He writes, 'But if Jesus is the anticipator of God, then he must simultaneously and unavoidably become the sign of resistance to the powers of a world which contradicts God and to the laws of a world which is closed to the future.'[12] In the ministry of Jesus, the Kingdom of God entered into history in a situation of conflict. So it will also be for those who try to follow him and enter into the praxis of discipleship. A concrete instance of this resistance would be the struggle to eliminate poverty. As Gutierrez has made clear, there are two types of poverty: the evangelical poverty of self-emptying and openness to God and the anti-evangelical poverty which kills. The follower of Christ is summoned to stand on the side of the poor against this lethal type of poverty.

To conclude these remarks on Moltmann's understanding of humanity's relation to the two cities, we might note its trinitarian character. According to Moltmann, the action of the Christian in the world is christologically founded, pneumatologically implemented and eschatologically oriented. Its foundations are in Christ's identification with the rejected and the Father's identification with him in God-forsakenness. It is implemented by the Spirit who creates signs of anticipation and resistance. It is oriented to the eschaton, when the Spirit's work will be completed and the Son will hand over the Kingdom to the Father, so that God will be all in all.

We might also note in passing that there is a great measure of agreement on this point between Moltmann's vision and that of liberation theologians. For liberation theology, the key problem of our epoch is the crisis of history and historical existence.[13] The massive disproportion between rich and poor, the enormous number of victims of war and famine, the threat of nuclear holocaust and the extinction of the human race, raise the question of the meaning of history in a radical way. How can history be meaningful if there is such vast suffering and senseless death? Liberation theologians do not doubt that ultimate salvation is trans-historical. But any attempt to preach this salvation which by-passes historical engagement falls prey to the Marxist charge of ideology. Thus they would affirm that salvation becomes concrete and real by on-going participation in the struggles of history. As Roger Haight puts it, 'Salvation is operative as a process of humanization or liberation within history.'[14] Or, as Sobrino urges, faith, hope and charity must become historical as God has become historical in Christ.[15] Thus, to return to the theme with which we opened this chapter, it is only in the historical praxis of following Christ, that we can know God.

Trinity, Monotheism and Monarchy

In discussing the relationship between Christian faith and praxis, we have thus far only adverted indirectly to the specifically trinitarian concept of God. This dimension however has become especially important since Erik Peterson's monograph *Monotheism as a Political Problem*.[16] This small study has an additional relevance since Peterson's ideas have been incorporated into Moltmann's political theology.[17]

Peterson's study showed that there has been a strong link historically between monotheism and monarchy. The religious conviction that there is only one God served to bolster the idea of one political ruler. As God guaranteed the unity of the cosmos, so the monarch guaranteed the unity of the state. Peterson showed how it was logical that the Arians, and in particular Eusebius, were the theologians of the Byzantine court. As Arians, they wanted to exclude the Logos from the Godhead and so preserve a simple and indivisible monarchy. These ideas naturally appealed to the emperor. As Peterson puts it, there was in this conception a perfect correspondence between the one and only king in heaven and the one and only king on earth.

According to Peterson, it was the supreme triumph of the early church to break with this type of monotheism. The development of the doctrine of the Trinity meant the end of all political theology. One could not appeal to religious ideology to bolster the government of the state. Christianity must never enter into an easy alliance with the rulers of this world.

How should Peterson's ideas be evaluated? I believe that there is need for a nuanced judgement. It is questionable whether the trinitarian character of God as such is the safe defence against despotic political systems. History does not generally witness to the fact that Christianity has been a critical force *vis-à-vis* political systems. One could also ask whether the monotheism of prophetic religion is not a sufficient guarantee against political despotism and against the exploitation of religion by political power.[18] Even in the Old Testament, the prophets showed a critical reserve toward the ambiguous value of the monarchy.

However, Peterson has made an important contribution in demonstrating that it is the eschatological dimension of Christianity which prevents any absolute identification between God and earthly kingdoms. The Christian eschatological hope renders all political powers provisional.

The other significant point to note is that, although Christians confess Jesus as king and messiah, this confession is based on the paschal mystery. Jesus is king by virtue of his resurrection, and the royal Psalm 110 was frequently applied to Jesus's resurrection. But one can never forget that this kingship is bound to his cross. Jesus comes to his Lordship through the mystery of the cross and even in his risen state he forever bears the marks of the passion in his body. Therefore, for a Christian, it is impossible to separate Christ's Kingship from his passion. This was the tragic mistake made by Christianity in the past when Christ the pantocrator was portrayed according to the model of the emperor. As Moltmann notes, 'The glory of the triune God is reflected, not in the crowns of kings and the triumphs of victors but in the face of the crucified Jesus, and in the faces of the oppressed whose brother he became.'[19] The cross becomes a permanent challenge to re-think the meaning of God's Lordship. It is true that God is Lord and almighty, but we cannot bring some *a priori* understanding of Lordship to clarify the nature of his omnipotence. Rather we have to think God's attributes in terms of his manifestation of himself. This God turns out to be the Father who identified himself with his crucified and rejected Son and poured out his Spirit from the cross as a source of hope for the God-forsaken of the earth.

Christological Identification

The key to Christian praxis is Christological identification. God has identified himself with Jesus who stood on the side of the poor, the emarginated and the God-forsaken. But where is the Christian to find Christ's presence in the world? The clear answer of scripture, as attested in the parable of the last judgment in Matthew 25, is in the least of his brethren.

One of the first features to note about this parable is its apocalyptic character. It is a scene of final judgment. Jesus is portrayed as the Son of Man who comes in judgment. John Donahue remarks[20] that apocalyptic scenes reveal transcendent values that should have been present before the final judgment. The message of the parable is that concrete actions of loving-kindness to those in need constitute the mercy which God desires and the criterion of his judgement.

A number of commentators have referred to the christological character of this parable.[21] We indicated above that Jesus is called Son of Man but he is also portrayed as king or messiah. In the Old Testament the king of Israel was meant to embody the attributes of God and we have seen that for Israel God was a God of justice with a special concern for the poor, the oppressed and the emarginated. Just as Jesus was God's justice incarnate, so his disciples will be judged by their readiness to follow him in living his new righteousness.

The striking feature of the parable is Christ's identification with the least of his brethren. As Moltmann says, the point of the parable is the presence of the coming judge now hidden in the poor. Thus a critical point for Jesus's followers is not whether they are willing to follow him but whether they have the eyes to see where he is present. As Donahue points out, the condemned in the parable:

> ... knew what justice demanded; they simply did not know or recognize where its demands were to be met in the world. In the scene it is the marginal and suffering in the world who reveal the place where the Son of Man, Lord and Judge, is, as it were, hidden in the world. The parable is a warning to Christians of all ages that they must discover not only what the doing of justice is but where justice is to be located.[22]

This final point, the 'where' of justice, leads us to ask who are the least of the brethren of Christ? Are they suffering and persecuted Christians or does the parable refer to all anonymous poor and suffering persons? Donahue argues[23] that in the context of Matthew's gospel the evangelist must be referring to suffering and persecuted Christians. If we link Matthew 25 and Matthew 28 where our Lord charges his disciples with the task of preaching the gospel to all nations, it becomes clear that the last judgement does not occur until the gospel has been preached to the whole world. Matthew is writing for a missionary church and part of its witness to the gospel must be readiness to suffer rejection and persecution. Donahue also shows that the sufferings of the least of Christ's brethren are remarkably like the apostolic sufferings which Paul underwent for the sake of the gospel and which he describes at length, especially in 2 Corinthians. However, Donahue sets us on guard lest we interpret this parable in a narrow sectarian way. The ethics proposed in the parable are the ethics of discipleship. Just as Christ identified with the poor and rejected, so any genuine disciple must make the same identification and must be prepared to face the same hostility. The sufferings which Christians undergo as a result of their witness of acts of loving-kindness to those in need are true testimony of authentic discipleship. Christians are living between the times. In the final judgement God will vindicate his church of suffering disciples. In the meantime, the faces of the poor and suffering reveal to the believer the presence of the final judge who is to come. Service to those in need constitutes both the criterion of final judgement and the measure of the church's authenticity in proclaiming God's will for all peoples.

Principles of Christian Praxis

To complete this chapter, it would be useful to sketch some principles of Christian praxis in their relation to the God who reveals himself in the life, death and resurrection of Jesus of Nazareth.

The first principle we could call the transcendent value of the human person. *Gaudium et Spes* enunciated this principle succinctly but beautifully when it stated, 'By his Incarnation the Son of God in a certain way united himself with every man.' (no. 22, 1). The same document goes on to affirm that 'the church is at once a sign and safeguard of the transcendent character of the human person.' (no. 76, 1). It is important, I believe, to stress the value of the word 'transcendent'. There is no doubt, in light of what we have already seen, that the church of Christ must be interested in the entire well-being of men and women. Salvation cannot be restricted to a so-called religious sphere. God wants to save the whole person. At the same time, concern for the wholeness of the person implies concern also for his or her transcendence. The human being can never be satisfied with anything less than God himself. Liberation in the economic sphere is truncated if it does not open a person to God who transcends inner-worldly fulfilment. As Paul VI expressed it in *Evangelii Nuntiandi*, ultimate salvation is transcendent and eschatological and consists in communion with God in eternity. He wrote:

> Liberation cannot be limited to any restricted sphere whether it be economic, political, social or cultural. It must rather take account of the totality of the human person in all its aspects and elements, including the openness of the human person to what is absolute, even to the Absolute, that is God. (no. 33, 1).

What is required here is what Donal Dorr calls an integral humanism.[24] This type of humanism refuses to bifurcate the human being into two departments, the spiritual and the temporal, which are opposed to each other. Rather an integral humanism respects the value of the social, the economic, the political and the cultural and sees them as contributing to the coming Kingdom of God. At the same time Christianity reminds human beings that their destiny lies beyond all these things in the transcendent God.

A second principle would be the social character of the person. One of the greatest negative inheritances of the Enlightenment is the idea of the subject as a private individual. According to Enlightenment thinking, the person is a self-possessing, self-disposing centre of action which sets itself apart from other persons. This leads to the view that the only value which is social is that which is marketable. All other values become purely private. Such a view of the person as purely functional and productive is thoroughly incompatible with God's christological identification with the poor and the outcast.

Both on philosophical and theological grounds, one could argue that there is no human subject that is not socially constituted. Many philosophers have shown that the I arises only in a dialogical situation where it is called into being by a Thou.[25] Hence it is not the case that there is first a fully constituted subject who subsequently puts himself into relationship with others. Rather the subject himself is thoroughly social. From a theological perspective the deepest reason for the human being's sociality is that the person is created in the image of the Trinity, the perfect community, where the three divine persons exist in an eternal self-giving. *Gaudium et Spes* hinted at this truth when it affirmed that there is such a likeness between the divine community and the human community that the human person is precisely that being who can realize himself only by giving himself away. The Council Fathers wrote:

> The Lord Jesus, when he prayed to the Father, 'that all may be one . . . as we are one' (John 17:21, 22) opened up vistas closed to human reason, for he implied a certain likeness between the union of the divine persons, and the unity of God's sons in truth and charity. This likeness reveals that man, who is the only creature on earth which God willed for itself, cannot fully find himself except through a sincere gift of himself. (no. 24, 2).

On these philosophical and theological grounds theologians today stress the social constitution of the person and the social dimension of human freedom. This view of the person leads to the praxis of solidarity which is the third principle which requires some elucidation.

Solidarity is a word which recalls humanity's basic vocation to unity and communion. For a Christian this solidarity is linked to narrative and memory. The Christian remembers the story of Jesus and of God's identification with the powerless and oppressed. On the basis of this memory the Christian wants to stand in solidarity with all those victims with whom God has identified himself in Christ. J. B. Metz puts it this way, 'The faith of Christians is a praxis in history and society that is to be understood as hope in solidarity in the God of Jesus Christ as God of the living and the dead who calls all men to be subjects in his presence.'[26]

The word 'solidarity' has the advantage that its connotations are thoroughly positive. It accentuates the human vocation to communion. In this context it is worth mentioning that it is in solidarity that we see the genuine meaning of freedom. Moltmann has pointed out that too often in Western thought freedom has been understood as lordship over another. I am free to the extent that I can control others. This conception of freedom leads to modern individualistic theories of the self and an understanding of society based on competition. But there is another understanding of freedom, according to which, the ideal of freedom is friendship. Friendship exists when there is both affection and respect. Hegel taught that friendship is the concrete concept of freedom. In this context, Moltmann writes, 'As long as freedom means lordship, everything has to be separated, isolated, detached and distinguished, so that it can be dominated. But if freedom means community, fellowship, then we experience the uniting of everything that has hitherto been separated.'[27] We have already seen that God has re-defined the idea of lordship by identifying himself with the crucified Christ. God has wanted to manifest his Lordship by becoming servant of all. And in Christ God has called us to the freedom of friendship: 'No longer do I call you servants, for the servant does not know what his master is doing; but I have called you friends, for all that I have heard from my Father I have made known to you.' (John 15:15).

What is the scope of this solidarity? Metz has said that it is both universal and partial. It is universal in the sense that God has called all men and women to community and friendship. But in light of the memory of the story of Jesus, Christian solidarity embraces in a special way the suffering of the world and the victims of oppression. But here again Christian solidarity is universal. It embraces even the dead, all those past victims of the human story of misery, and includes them in the hope of the new creation and the coming kingdom of righteousness. At the same time, Christian solidarity is particular. It does not remain an abstract love of humanity but identifies with the poor and the suffering close at hand.

One should also note that solidarity is an active word. To be sure, solidarity first connotes identification with others, but it also connotes the active struggle to rid the world of suffering, to fight the forces of death and free the oppressed from injustice. Solidarity therefore implies a commitment to the ongoing process of liberation. The word solidarity plays an especially important role in the social teaching of Pope John Paul II as is witnessed by its prominence in *Laborem Exercens*, his encyclical letter on work (see no. 8, 1; 8, 3f.). Donal Dorr points out that in the thinking of the Pope solidarity plays a role similar to that of class struggle in Marxist thought.[28] John Paul II rejects the notion of class struggle, for it is based on a philosophy of violence. Its philosophical anthropology is too negative. According to John Paul II, solidarity does not imply the struggle of one group of people or one class against another. At the same time, as I indicated above, solidarity is an active word. It does imply a struggle for justice. The Pope envisages the possibility of a justified reaction of workers against an unjust and exploitative system. Solidarity is thus a word which gives scope to legitimate opposition and confrontation while at the same time preserving the focus that the ultimate goal of such struggle is unity and community.

As a fourth principle I would enunciate the thesis that 'concern for justice is an intrinsic and constitutive element or form of Christian faith.'[29] This principle was given official endorsement by the Catholic Church in the statement of the Synod of Bishops of 1971, *Proclaiming Justice and Peace*, where the bishops state, 'Action on behalf of justice and participation in the transformation of the world fully appear to us as a constitutive dimension of the preaching of the gospel, or, in other words, of the church's mission for the redemption of the human race and its liberation from every oppressive situation.' (no. 6). The first thing to be noted about this statement is the word 'constitutive'. The bishops are so linking the struggle for justice with faith that there is no authentic faith without a corresponding commitment to create the conditions of justice. This idea is also in keeping with our initial reflection about theory and praxis. Christianity is a form of liberating praxis in the world. Without this praxis, faith becomes an ideology. Through an authentic faith, however, one comes to know God concretely as one discovers his presence in the suffering faces of Christ's exploited brothers and sisters.

The second point to note is the relation between love and justice. In the same document of the 1971 Synod the bishops state, 'Christian love of neighbour and justice cannot be separated. For love implies an absolute demand for justice, namely a recognition of the dignity and rights of one's neighbour.' (no. 34). Roger Haight develops this point when he explains that justice is not added to love, rather justice is the medium of love, it is the structure through which love becomes operative in the world. Haight goes on to explain that justice is ontological, for justice means responding to realities for what they are. Since we have already spoken of the Christian commitment to the transcendent value of every person and to freedom as the goal of human solidarity, justice can be seen as the form of love that corresponds to the equality, dignity and freedom of persons. But here again this justice cannot be understood in a private or individualistic sense but must be incarnated in the social structures of reality. In today's world it is often the social structures that cause the gravest injustice.

As a final principle we may state the thesis that 'mercy completes the meaning of justice by preventing justice from shutting itself up within the circle of revenge.'[30] This principle has been developed most beautifully by Pope John Paul II in his encyclical letter, *Dives in Misericordia* where the Pope meditates upon the parable of the prodigal son (see nos. 5–6). If the father in the parable had limited himself merely to justice, he would have reduced the son to the status of a hired servant. But the father remains faithful to his vocation and so restores to his son the dignity of his sonship. Because of the father's mercy, the son's lost humanity is restored. From this we see that the norm of justice, taken as absolute, is too narrow. It needs to be open to the gift of mercy. What binds the one who shows mercy to the one who has violated justice is their common humanity. The one who is forgiven is not made to feel humiliated. Rather his humanity is restored to value. As the Pope points out (no. 12, 2), the statement that mercy transcends justice does not detract from the value of justice or minimize the significance of the order that is based upon it, but rather the transcendence of mercy indicates that the human spirit from which justice flows contains other resources of humanity which are even more profound.

Conclusion

Underlying the thought of this chapter has been the trenchant objection of Kant that belief in the Trinity has no practical consequences for human life. The burden of the argument has been that the opposite is the case, for the Christian account of God is rooted in the story of Jesus. The doctrine of the Trinity is the hermeneutic of the cross. Christianity lives from the memory of one in whom God's new righteousness has appeared, one who identified with the poor and the outcast even to the point of a God-forsaken death on the cross. But the resurrection has revealed that God has made Jesus's identification his own. To know Jesus and the God he called Father is therefore only possible by the Spirit of Jesus poured out from the cross, who sets one on a journey of discipleship. Only in serving the least of Christ's brothers and sisters can one recognize the presence of God in this world and be judged worthy to enter the Kingdom when the humiliated Christ comes in glory as the triumphant Son of Man.

IX

Trinitarian Prayer

Introduction

Peter Faber, one of the first companions of St Ignatius Loyola, defined Christian prayer in this way: in the Spirit to ask the Father for the Son. In the light of our reflections in this book such a definition is not surprising because we have seen that the essential structure of Christian revelation and Christian faith are trinitarian. In Chapter 2, I indicated how faith as a response to revelation corresponds to the trinitarian structure of revelation. Faith, we saw, was no mere act of the intellect but a response of the whole person, an existential act, an act of commitment and trust by which one responds to God's revelation in Christ. Faith allows us to participate in this revelation-event so that we share the divine life. Only God can make faith possible since only God divinizes us. Hence faith is made possible by the action of the Holy Spirit in us.

I see the relationship between faith and prayer as the relation of the implicit and the explicit. Through my baptism I share in God's trinitarian life, and from day-to-day in trying to live out my Christian commitment I am implicitly actualizing my faith. My life in the world, as St Paul says, is oriented to be a sacrifice of praise to the Father through the Son in the Holy Spirit. (Rom. 12:1). However, this implicit worship of my life comes to explicit expression in my prayer, whether it be the liturgical prayer of the church or my own personal prayer. A helpful analogy here is the relationship between human love and its bodily expression. A reflection on human being in the world indicates that human subjectivity never exists in a disincarnate way. I can only be a subject by expressing myself in the world, by concrete actions, signs and gestures. Apart from these concretizations of myself, I cannot exist nor can I be accessible to others. When I love another person, that love naturally wishes to express itself in signs and gestures. A husband can love his wife, can offer himself to her and be faithful to her without ever kissing her. A married couple can pledge themselves to each other without physical intercourse. But these human, bodily gestures render their love concrete. The language of the body not only expresses their love but through this expression their love is deepened and intensified.

So it is with prayer. It seems to me inappropriate to ask why a person should pray, why prayer is necessary. Prayer is a spontaneous overflow of the life of faith. The primacy is always with God's act of revelation, his offer of himself in Jesus Christ and our surrender to that offer made possible by the Spirit. This act of faith, however, inevitably expresses itself in the language of prayer. I cannot help but make explicit that which is happening at the deepest level of my being. The faith dimension of my life overflows in the signs and gestures of worship and in the language of prayer.

The Trinitarian Structure of Christian Prayer

It might be useful to reflect for a few moments on how authentic Christian prayer is of its very nature radically trinitarian. Hans Urs von Balthasar has been one of the most important spiritual writers in this century to stress this point. As early as his magisterial work on Christian contemplation in 1957, he demonstrated that our capacity for contemplation is founded in the Father, the Son and the Holy Spirit.[1] According to Balthasar there are two minimal conditions for the possibility of prayer, that the hidden eternal God is open to the human person and that the person is in turn open to God. His latest work on Christian meditation (1984) begins with the sentence, 'The absolutely decisive question is whether God has spoken to man – i.e. spoken about himself and about his purpose in creating the world and humankind – or whether the Absolute remains silent beyond all worldly words.'[2]

The decisive point then is that God has spoken. God has addressed us and the human person is created by God as dialogical. The human being is created by God to be addressed. Faith is receptivity to this word. This receptivity becomes explicit in the language of prayer. If I know who and what I really am (God's dialogical partner), I will burst spontaneously into the prayer of praise and thanksgiving.

Balthasar reflects at length on how this speech of God and the human response to it reflects the trinitarian being of God. The Father is the origin and ultimate source of this dialogue. He is the ultimate principle of freedom and election. Within the Godhead, the Father is pure address, so much so that he expresses himself perfectly as Word. The Father's I meets his perfect response in the

Thou of the Son. However, the dialogue which the Father initiates within the divine life is not closed in upon itself. It is essentially open – open to humanity – open to creation, to time and to history. In the Father's eternal freedom he determines himself to be a God of men and women, to be our God. The eternal election of the Son includes our election. As Ephesians expresses it, 'In Christ he chose us before the world was founded, to be dedicated, to be without blemish in his sight, to be full of love; and he destined us – such was his will and pleasure – to be accepted as his sons through Jesus Christ, in order that the glory of his gracious gift, so graciously bestowed on us in his Beloved, might redound to his praise.' (Eph. 1:3–5).

The Father is eternally open to us. He does not wish to remain a hidden God but to show us his face. What he has to say to us is made visible in the Son. It is the fourth gospel especially which meditates upon this truth. At the conclusion of the prologue, the evangelist writes, 'No one has ever seen God; but God's only Son, who is nearest to the Father's heart, he has made him known.' (Jn. 1:18). The Greek verb *exēgēsato*, which the evangelist employs in this verse, is quite interesting. Literally it means that the Son is the exegesis of the Father – the Son interprets the Father to us. With Balthasar, we can say that the Son is the mediation of the Father to us. Without this mediation we have no access to the Father. On the other hand, because of the identity of the word which Jesus addresses to us with his person, his entire being is revelatory. In every dimension of his being he is Word – he is expressive of the Father. Thus there is nothing about the Son, no word or gesture, which does not concern me. As Jesus expresses it later in the fourth gospel, 'He who sees me sees the Father.' (Jn. 14:9).

This is an important point, stressed by such contemporary theologians as Karl Rahner and Balthasar. Rahner affirms that the humanity of Christ is of permanent significance for faith.[3] Our journey to the Father is always mediated by the Son, and indeed by the Son in his humanity. The humanity which Jesus assumed in the Incarnation has not been discarded in the resurrection and ascension. Jesus is glorified at the right hand of the Father in his humanity. Rahner concludes that even in the beatific vision we will see God through the humanity of Jesus. Balthasar argues that here we see the ground of Christian contemplation and the distinguishing mark of Christian prayer, Christian prayer is both made possible by and is bound to the Word.

Here of course we must distinguish various senses of the meaning of the Word of God. Naturally the Word of God in the primordial sense is Jesus Christ himself. For a Christian, prayer is essentially directed to the Father through this Word. Another important sense of the Word of God is scripture. As Karl Barth says,[4] this is God's Word in a derivative sense. The scripture cannot be directly identified with revelation but the scripture is inspired so that God can speak to us through this Word. In this sense the scripture can be revelation for us.

The Second Vatican Council quotes the remark of St Jerome that ignorance of the scriptures is ignorance of Christ.[5] The Council wanted to overcome a one-sided sacramental piety by emphasizing that the church receives the bread of life from both the table of the Word and the table of the Eucharist. The Council went on to say that the inspired scriptures impart the Word of God without change.[6] Here, one way to understand prayer would be simply receptivity to the Word. Prayer is not primarily an activity or a doing, but fundamentally a receptivity. Prayer is an opening of the heart to receive God's Word. The history of God's dialogue with his people is a prolonged heart-felt cry, 'If today you hear his voice, harden not your hearts.' (Ps. 95:7–8). The culmination of this history is God's offer of his Word in the Incarnation. Here God met the perfect prayer in Mary's *fiat*. Her Yes to God, her receptivity was an opening of her womb to receive the seed of God's Word. Theologians such as Balthasar stress that all prayer has essentially this Marian structure of receptivity to the Word. Another symbol of this profound truth can be found in the story of Martha and Mary in Luke 10. It was Origen who first saw in this narrative a parable of the active and contemplative life. However, it is probably truer to say that Luke is not praising the contemplative life above the active one. The one thing necessary here is listening to the Word of God. The Mary of this story is praised because she is listening to God's Word and according to Luke such listening is indispensable both for active people and so-called contemplatives. As Jesus puts it in Chapter 8 of Luke's gospel, 'My mother and brethren are those who hear the Word of God and do it.' (Lk. 8:21).

Before leaving this point, I believe that it is worth noting

Balthasar's insistence that the Christian's life with the Word is the decisive point which distinguishes Christian prayer from all other types of prayer. This point follows naturally from the unique foundation of Christian experience, namely that God has spoken. Hence God is ever to be found in his Word and this Word can never be by-passed. The danger of by-passing the Word is the danger of all types of mysticism. There are many types of natural mysticism as well as some mystical traditions of Oriental religions which seek a union with Being, Reality or Nothing (or whatever word one uses to describe the goal of this human longing), which leaves all worldly realities behind and in which the self is dissolved. Also in the Christian tradition, under the influence of some philosophical traditions, the goal of prayer has been seen to be a falling into a nameless abyss. According to this interpretation the highest type of prayer and the only genuine experience of God is the *via negativa*. Christianity, however, is an incarnational faith and therefore, as we have seen, any prayer which seeks to leave God's Word behind, is counterfeit.

For some pages now we have been stressing the christological character of prayer and this is natural. However, to complete the picture and to avoid the extreme of christomonism, we must refer to the Holy Spirit, for, as we have said, the condition of possibility of Christian prayer is trinitarian. The simple fact is that God's Word would be a mere historical event of the past if it were not for the Holy Spirit who makes Christ contemporary and lets him speak to us today. It is, in short, the pneumatic Christ who addresses us. Moreover, as we have seen, our response to the Word would not be possible without the action of the Spirit within us. Paradoxically, our receptivity to God's Word is both an act of our freedom and the enabling action of the Holy Spirit within us. As St Paul says in 1 Corinthians (2:10), 'The Spirit explores everything, even the depths of God's own nature.' Hence it is up to the Spirit to open us to the depths of the divine life. As we noted earlier, the condition of possibility of contemplation is not only God's openness to us but our openness to him. Our ability to receive his Word as something alive within us is due to the Spirit's action. Thus, as the author of Ephesians writes, 'Give yourselves wholly to prayer and to entreaty: pray on every occasion in the power of the Spirit.' (Eph. 6:18).

In this way we see how the life of prayer exists within a trinitarian circle. Its origin is the Father's love and election of us. This love comes to visible expression in God's ikon, his Word of life, Jesus Christ. The Word becomes alive within us by the Spirit. ('Were not our hearts burning within us while he talked to us on the road and opened to us the scriptures?' Lk. 24:32) As Balthasar writes,

> Contemplation is made possible, insofar as it is prepared by God – by the Father who predestines, chooses and accepts us as his sons; by the Son, who makes known to us the Father, and gives himself to us in his self-giving unto death and the Eucharistic mystery; by the Holy Spirit, who brings and makes known to our soul the divine life.[7]

The Pilgrimage of Prayer

The great spiritual traditions of both East and West indicate that the life of prayer is not static but is a pilgrimage. There is a natural progression, as one is led by God to an ever greater union with himself. In his little study on prayer,[8] Franz Jalics indicates four stages of the pilgrimage. The first is vocal prayer. We learn to pray as we learn to talk, by being taught what to say. A second stage is more intellectual. The mind comes into play during prayer. One reflects upon a passage of scripture and this reflection opens the person to a prayerful response to God speaking through the Word. Jalics distinguishes a third stage when one enters into spontaneous conversation with the Lord about one's life, one's problems and sufferings, one's joys and hopes. A figure such as Job comes to mind here. The last stage of the pilgrimage is sheer surrender to the Lord in silence. Here words are no longer important. In a human relationship, the beginning stages are often characterized by much conversation, and silences are often awkward, but as the relationship grows, one takes the other for granted. After many years of marriage one is often content just to be in the presence of the other person without saying anything. So it is with prayer. As one enters into contemplation, one learns to be rather than to speak. A number of other authors speak of this pilgrimage as a journey from the lips, to the mind, to the heart. God is ultimately interested in the heart and wants to lead the believer to the point where the heart quietly abides in him.

In this section I would like to say a few words about this prayer of the heart, the culmination of contemplation, and indicate how this prayer can also be seen to manifest the trinitarian character of all Christian prayer. Many contemporary Christians are rediscovering their vocation to be contemplatives and an ever greater number of Christians are being led to contemplative prayer. Authors such as William Johnston, Basil Pennington, John Main, Kallistos Ware[9] and many others have helped us to rediscover the Eastern tradition of hesychasm and the tradition of *The Cloud of Unknowing* in the West. The accent in these traditions is on simplicity, on a non-verbal and non-conceptual abiding in the Lord. Jalics defines contemplation as a loving glance at God without words, thoughts or rational analysis. In the same way Pennington speaks of prayer as a state of loving attention.

The author of *The Cloud* offers us a means to facilitate this attention. He suggests that we choose a short word, a word that is meaningful to us. Then we should fix our minds on this word, so that our attention may be centred in this word, come what may. In chapter 40 he advises, 'Let this little word represent to you God in all his fullness and nothing less than the fullness of God. Let nothing except God hold sway in your mind and heart.'

Combining these insights with the great hesychastic tradition of Eastern Christianity, we can say that there is no more suitable word than the name of our saviour Jesus Christ, whom, we have seen, is our mediator to the Father and who represents all that the Father wants to say to us. The mysticism of the name of Jesus has a firm biblical foundation. In Acts 4:12 we read, 'There is no other name under heaven by which we must be saved.' Likewise, in Paul's magnificent hymn in Philippians 2, he exclaims, 'At the name of Jesus every knee shall bow, of those in heaven, on earth and under the earth and every tongue shall confess that Jesus Christ is Lord, to the glory of the Father.' (vs. 10–11). This hymn praising the name of Jesus has as its setting the kenosis or self-emptying of Jesus. Paul exhorts his readers to have that mind which was in Christ, i.e., that attitude of self-emptying. Every time we centre our prayer on the name, we empty ourselves of our egoism, our I-centredness and let Christ become the centre of our being.

The proven experience of at least 1,500 years is that the repetition of the name can lead us into the experience of a deep union with Christ and through him with the Father. This contemplative tradition known as the Jesus prayer can exist in a variety of forms. In its classical form, the Christian prays, 'Lord Jesus, Son of God, be merciful to me a sinner.' Kallistos Ware points out that this simple aspiration contains implicitly the entire trinitarian faith of the church. Jesus is invoked as Son of God and hence there is an implicit recognition of his Father. Jesus's identity cannot be separated from the Father whose Son he is. Likewise there is an implicit recognition of the Spirit, because we call Jesus Lord, and as St Paul says, 'No one can say Jesus is Lord except in the Holy Spirit.' (1 Cor. 12:3).

However, many Christians will prefer an even simpler formulation and invoke only the name of Jesus or the fuller confession Jesus Christ. But here as well, there is an implicit trinitarian structure to our prayer even if that prayer consists in only one word. To my mind, this is most clearly seen when one links the Jesus prayer to the high-priestly prayer of Christ in the seventeenth chapter of the gospel of St John.

The theme of this chapter is struck in the first verse: glory, the glory of the Son and of the Father. Jesus prays that the Father will glorify him and give him that glory which he had before the foundation of the world. Jesus's whole life has consisted in doxology, in praising and glorifying his Father. Now he prays that through his paschal mystery he be led to the fullness of eschatological glory. The glory of Jesus is not, however, something for his own possession only. Jesus has come to share his glory. Thus the seventeenth chapter associates glory with eternal life and Jesus affirms, 'This is eternal life, that they know thee the only true God, and Jesus Christ whom thou hast sent.' (v. 3). As Walter Kasper notes,[10] knowledge here is not a mere abstract intellectual knowledge, but the knowledge of participation, union and love. Thus the seventeenth chapter has two parts: there is the prayer of praise, followed by the prayer of petition. The first flows over into the second, because Jesus wants his disciples to share in his glory and in the fullness of life which he possesses as Son. The culmination of the chapter, then, can be seen in Verse 21. Here is the goal of Jesus's saving work: 'That they may all be one; even as thou, Father, art in me, and I in thee, that they also may be one in us, so that the world may believe that thou hast sent me.'

A key word earlier in the Last Supper discourse was 'abide'. Using the analogy of the vine and the branches, Jesus exhorts his disciples to abide in his love. The full trinitarian meaning of this abiding is revealed in chapter seventeen. When praying the name of Jesus, one's loving attention is focused on him. But Jesus is not the goal in himself. He is always the mediator, pointing beyond himself to the Father. If we abide in him as we focus on his name, we ultimately abide in the Father, for Jesus is in the Father and the Father is in him. Moreover, this is not a mere binitarianism, for the Spirit is always the condition of possibility of Jesus's being in us. In the whole Last Supper discourse, the Spirit is never absent. In fact the whole of the second half of John's gospel is concerned with the sending of another paraclete who has the task of recalling and making present the work of Christ. Thus the abiding in Christ and in the Father is essentially linked to the presence of the Spirit within us. For me this is powerfully symbolized by the human breath which is evocative of the Holy Spirit whom scripture describes as the breath of God. In the tradition of hesychasm, the evocation of the name is usually co-ordinated with the rhythm of the breath. Theologically we could see this as the Holy Spirit breathing within us the name of Jesus, making him present so that we abide in him and in union with him abide in the Father. In this way the contemplative tradition of the Jesus prayer can be seen to point to the deepest mystery of faith, the union of the believer with the life of the Trinity, as Jesus says, 'Thou Father in me and I in them.'

Three Images of Prayer

It is impossible to speak of our pilgrimage to God without the help of images. Already in speaking of the conditions of contemplation, we used the image of listening to the Word. And in defining the nature of contemplation, we suggested the image of a loving glance at God. In the preceding reflections we appealed to the fourth gospel as the culmination of the contemplative vision, the reciprocal union of Christ and the Father, the believer and Christ. Without adding anything theological to what has preceded, we might be able to render the nature of prayer more concrete by referring to three incidents in the synoptic gospels which can illumine the meaning of prayer as loving attention.

Perhaps we can begin with an image of contrast found in the story of the pharisee and the publican (Lk. 18:9–14). The publican's prayer is the foundation for the tradition of the Jesus-prayer. His is a prayer for mercy: God, be merciful to me a sinner. He is a perfect symbol of loving attention to God. His prayer is completely devoid of egocentricity. The pharisee's prayer by contrast is egocentric: 'I fast twice a week, I give tithes of all that I get.' He has completely failed to grasp the attitude of self-emptying. He is so full of himself that he has no room in his heart to receive anything as a gift. Moreover, his prayer is based on contrasts and comparisons. 'God, I thank thee that I am not like other men.' The prayer of the true contemplative, on the contrary, overflows in love and compassion. Realizing one's need before God, his heart is open to the needs of others. The self-emptying, which opens one to God, opens one as well to an acceptance of one's neighbour. The closed heart of the pharisee leads rather to exclusion. By contrast, the contemplative's union with Christ gives him a shared identity. As Basil Pennington notes, there is no fragility here. There is strength in unity. No room is left for competition. Pennington goes on to cite the experience of Thomas Merton as recorded in his journal. 'Thank God, thank God, that I *am* like other men, that I am only a man among others . . . It is a glorious distinction to be a member of the human race.'[11]

The same contemplative attitude as the publican's is expressed in another story in St Luke's gospel, that of the woman who is a sinner in chapter 7 (vs. 36–50). Here again we see the same contrast between the woman and Simon the pharisee. Simon, realizing that the woman is a prostitute, sets himself above her and refuses to share a meal of fellowship with her. The woman, knowing who she is, does not seek to hide her identity but brings all that she is before Jesus. Weeping she bathes his feet with her tears and wipes them with her hair before anointing them with oil. The striking aspect of this scene is the openness with which she approaches Jesus. There is no attempt to hide who she is, to disguise her real identity. It is a common experience of the mystics that in genuine prayer God not only reveals who he is but who we are. If we really try to abide in him in radical simplicity, the true nature of ourselves will be revealed to us. Thus the testimony of the whole mystical tradition is that the road to union can only be through purification. Unfortunately we human beings often have the tendency to repress our true selves. In prayer we often bring to the Lord a false image of ourselves, the self we would like to be rather than the self we are. The woman of Luke 7 is a powerful testimony that we can dare to bring our true selves to contemplation with all our darknesses, our unbelief, our anger, our boredom, our disappointment, our feelings of inferiority. If we dare to abide in him as we are, his burning light will purify our darkness. His promise is that through this purification there will come about a radiant union. St John of the Cross says that we are like a damp log of wood. When the fire is lit in it, first its dampness makes it smoulder and crackle, but when it is dried, a white-hot fire glows within it.

The final image of the contemplative is also from St Luke's gospel. It is the parable of the watchful servant (chapter 12:35–40). In the parable, the servant's master is off to a marriage feast. The servant does not know when he will return, but his love keeps him vigilant. The servant is not concerned to do anything. He is merely there, watchful, ready. His concern is only with waiting. The Master will come when he is ready, whether in the first, the second or the third watch. The servant is not anxious to hurry him. But when the Master comes and knocks, the servant is ready to receive him. In other images, we have seen the contemplative as listening to the Word or glancing at the Lord. Here the image is of waiting. It is the same image as that of the sentinel in Psalm 130: 'More than the watchman waits for the dawn, so my soul waits for the Lord.' The psalmist continues, 'My soul waits for the Lord and in his Word I hope.' Such is the attitude of the Christian contemplative. Balthasar spoke of contemplation as abiding in the Word. Here in the image of Luke 12 and Psalm 130, it is the image of waiting upon the Word, the Word who is Christ – God's speech to us.

The Eucharist as a Trinitarian Event

In Chapter IV on the paschal mystery, I endeavoured to show that the paschal mystery must be interpreted as an event involving the Father, the Son and the Holy Spirit. Thus far in this chapter, we have discussed the trinitarian character of contemplation. The test of this interpretation is the liturgical prayer of the church, since here the church as such is at prayer. It is my contention that in fact in the sacraments and especially in the Eucharist the trinitarian character of prayer becomes most evident. Nowhere is this clearer than in the Eucharistic prayer itself. Since the Eucharist is the representation of the paschal mystery, this is exactly what we would expect.

The Second Vatican Council in a number of texts stressed the trinitarian character of the Eucharist. In no. 47 of the Constitution on the Liturgy, the Council Fathers wrote:

> From the time of Pentecost ... the Church has never failed to come together to celebrate the paschal mystery ... celebrating the Eucharist in which the victory and triumph of Christ's death are again made present and at the same time giving thanks to God for his unspeakable gift in Christ Jesus, to the praise of his glory, through the power of the Holy Spirit.

In another document, that on the priesthood, the Council states:

> The most blessed Eucharist contains the church's entire spiritual wealth, i.e. Christ himself our passover and living bread. Through his very flesh, made vital and vitalizing by the Holy Spirit, he offers life to men. They are thereby invited and led to offer themselves, their labours, and all created things together with him.[12]

In his authoritative work *Theological Dimensions of the Liturgy*, Vagaggini shows that the Trinity forms the basis of all liturgical prayer. Naturally the liturgy is not interested in a speculative grasp of the inner life of the Trinity. But the presence of the Trinity is felt in the key prepositions 'a', 'per', 'in', and 'ad'. Everything comes from the Father and returns to him. Liturgical prayer is always addressed to the Father. However, the prayer is addressed to the Father *per Filium*, through the mediation of the Son, and the action is performed in the Holy Spirit. There are three great testimonies to the presence of the Trinity in the mass. First, Vagaggini points out that the 'Deus' to whom the orations of the mass are addressed is the Father. Such prayers normally end with a reference to the mediation of the Son, *per Christum Dominum nostrum*. A second important witness is the doxology at the end of the eucharistic prayer. Finally, there is the structure of the anaphora itself. Vagaggini writes, 'The Father appears as the *principium quo* and the *terminus ad quem* of the Eucharistic action. Christ, the incarnate Son, appears there as the High Priest, *through* whom we perform the same priestly action. The Holy Spirit appears there as the *in quo*, He in whose presence the same action is completed *hic et nunc*.'[13]

The Christian understanding of God has always acknowledged the two sendings of the Father, by which God reveals himself, that of the Son and that of the Holy Spirit. The mission of the Son is obviously at the centre of the eucharistic prayer. The eucharist is first and foremost an act of memory. The church praises the Father for his great saving deeds in history culminating in the salvific act *par excellence*, the death and resurrection of Christ. The Catholic tradition, especially in the West, has stressed the sacrificial character of the eucharist. Christ himself is the priest as well as the victim in the eucharist. The ordained priest who offers the mass acts *in persona Christi*. Western Christianity's understanding of the eucharist is typically christological, and because of the controversies at the time of the Reformation, the Catholic tradition has stressed the words of consecration pronounced by the priest and the resulting transubstantiation.

Today, especially in the light of ecumenical dialogue not only with Protestantism but also with the great tradition of Eastern Orthodoxy, we see that the West's eucharistic theology is one-sided. First of all, there is recognition today that one should not rigidly limit the moment of consecration to the words of institution. The early church recognized the whole anaphora as consecratory. Secondly, we must be cautious of the danger of christomonism. Although Christ is the High Priest and although the ordained priest acts in the person of Christ, this must not be understood so as to exclude the role of the Holy Spirit. As Congar makes clear, it is the pneumatic Christ who acts in the eucharist, and the body of Christ which we receive in the eucharist is the Easter, pneumatic Christ, i.e. Christ penetrated by the Holy Spirit.[14]

If we look back to the Fathers of the church, we can see that it would be false to neglect either the christological or the pneumatic aspect of the eucharist or to create an opposition between them. As in the history of salvation, so in the sacraments, and in the eucharist in particular, the two missions are complementary. Congar appeals, for example, to Augustine who writes, 'The consecration which makes the Eucharist such a great sacrament comes only from the invisible action of the Spirit of God.'[15] Likewise Augustine exhorts his flock: 'Let us not eat the flesh of Christ and the blood of Christ only in sign, but let us eat and drink unto the participation in the Spirit.'[16] Such is also the theology of the Eastern church. The purpose of the epiclesis is that the elements be sanctified and so become the body of Christ, but beyond this that the communion in the body of Christ take its effect in the faithful. The purpose of Holy Communion is not just a physical sharing in the Body of Christ. The purpose is the divinization of the believer, the union of the believer with the Father through Christ, but also the union of believers with one another. The fruit of the eucharist is meant to be the unity of the Mystical Body. The eucharist can only produce all these desired effects through the action of the Holy Spirit.

In summary then, we can say that the eucharist as the culmination of the church's prayer and as the representation of the paschal mystery bears witness to the complementary action of the Son and the Spirit in their respective missions from the Father. Through these missions the Father is made known to us and we are divinized as we are drawn into the trinitarian economy of salvation. Louis Bouyer sums up beautifully the complementarity of the missions of the Son and the Spirit in the eucharist.

> The consecrator of all these Eucharists is always Christ alone, the Word made flesh, insofar as he is ever the dispenser of the Spirit because he handed himself over to death and then rose from the dead by the power of the same Spirit. But in the indivisible totality of the Eucharist, this Word, evoked by the church, and her own prayer calling for the fulfilment of the Word through the power of the Spirit, come together for the mysterious fulfilment of the divine promises.[17]

X

God and World in Trinitarian Perspective

The Creation

The problem which I propose to examine in this chapter is the God-world relation. In what perspective should this relation be understood? Is a trinitarian perspective the one which ultimately renders this relationship intelligible?

First of all, we can recall that the perspective of classical philosophical theism is generally recognized as inadequate to clarify our problem. Kasper notes[1] that the unipersonal God of theism is untenable for a variety of reasons. First, if God is thought of as the ultimate counterpart of man, in spite of the personal categories we use to describe him, he is ultimately reduced to the supreme object, to a supreme being who is superior to all other beings. This type of God, in the long run, arouses the atheistic critique in the name of human autonomy. On the other hand, such a theistic God needs the human being as his covenant partner in order to realize himself. If God is a unipersonal God and if we want to say that this God is love, then God needs humanity as a partner to realize his own nature. God would create out of need; hence his relation to the world would be necessary rather than free and gratuitous.

In light of these objections, many Christian theologians today argue that only a trinitarian perspective can shed light on the God-world relationship. In his *magnum opus*, *Theodramatik*, Hans Urs von Balthasar notes that only the mystery of the Trinity can enable us to avoid two false interpretations of the world.[2] On the one hand, the atheistic interpretation reduces the being of the world to a worthless fact which exists merely as raw material for human action. On the other hand, theism reduces the world to a worthless non-fact, for outside of the Absolute, apparently nothing can really exist or be given as a gift.

Later in the same work, Balthasar recalls that the classical theology of the Middle Ages always attempted to reflect on the creation within the mystery of the Trinity. Bonaventure taught, for example, that God could not have created creatures by his will if he had not already generated the Son by his nature.[3] Thomas Aquinas taught the same doctrine. He wrote, 'From the procession of the distinct divine persons every procession and multiplicity of creatures is caused.'[4] And in another place he teaches that the Son lets streams flow from himself into the creation. Clarifying this point, Aquinas observes, 'I understand these streams as currents of the eternal procession, by which the Son proceeds from the Father, and the Holy Spirit from the Father and the Son in an ineffable manner.'[5] Here we see that St Thomas closely links together the creation and the eternal processions.

Taking this classical tradition as our clue, how can we understand the relation between the Trinity and the creation? Perhaps, first of all, we can say a word about the 'place' of the creation. Here I would like to appropriate the insight of Balthasar that the 'place' of the creation is the trinitarian life itself. There is no 'outside' of the Trinity. Outside of the triune life there is nothing. Thus the place of the creation must be within the inner-trinitarian relations. We have already seen (in Chapter IV) on the paschal mystery that the Father's whole being consists in giving himself to the Son. The Father's self-gift opens a space for the Son. Father and Son exist in an eternal *diastasis*. However, since the Father's offer is perfectly responded to by the Son, the *diastasis* is bridged over by the Holy Spirit. The Holy Spirit as bond of love both holds open and bridges over the *diastasis* between the Father and the Son. Precisely in this *diastasis* is the 'place' of the creation. The Father holds nothing back but gives himself away. The Father risks himself in freedom on the Son. The Son too in perfect freedom responds to the Father's love. Thus the *diastasis* between the Father and the Son is a *diastasis* of freedom and love. In this *diastasis* there is room for genuine created freedom. This *diastasis* is not a threat to human autonomy but the condition of its possibility.

An important consideration here is that the love of the Father and the Son is an open love, not a love closed in upon itself. In the words of Adrienne von Speyr, the love of the Father, the Son and the Holy Spirit is wide enough to embrace the whole world.[6] Another image which may help here is that of the Holy Spirit as the divine ecstasy of love. In Western trinitarian theology, the Holy Spirit is the *vinculum amoris*, but precisely as bond of a genuine, non-egoistic love, the Holy Spirit is ecstatic. God's love overflows, making place for the creation and history. The divine drama of love opens out to the drama between God and the world, God and humanity. Already within this perspective, the conundrum of theism is surpassed. God is neither supreme object over against humanity nor the supreme Thou depending on the human I for fulfilment. God is in his own life interpersonal communion, and because God in his own being is love, God can be love for us, a love which is free and gratuitous. The love which God *is* overflows into creation and time.

The second point which is critical here is that the creation is christologically determined. In numerous texts of the scripture, we see that the New Testament thinks of the creation in christological terms. There is, for example, the vision of the creation which we find at the beginning of the Letter to the Ephesians, 'God chose us in him before the foundation of the world, that we should be holy and blameless before him. He destined us in love to be his sons through Jesus Christ, according to the purpose of his will.' (Eph. 1:4–5). A similar vision is found in the hymn of Colossians (chapter 1:15–20) where the author affirms that all things in heaven and on earth were created through Christ and for Christ. According to this hymn, Christ is not only the source of the unity of the creation but the head of the church as well. The goal of God's work in creation is thus Christ and the church. Creation finds its fulfilment when all men and women are incorporated into Christ and into his church, which is his body. As Balthasar notes,[7] whatever may be the origin of this hymn, the author has given it a dynamic-historical interpretation. The God-world relationship is not thought of statically but historically. Creation is the first step and an inner-moment of God's historical action of giving himself totally to the world in Christ and leading the world through his Son back to union with himself.

To further elucidate this point, we can introduce the useful suggestion of Karl Barth and Karl Rahner regarding the relationship between creation and redemption. Barth expresses it this way: the creation is the external ground of the covenant; the covenant is the internal ground of the creation. This is to say that God from all eternity has been the God of the covenant, the God who has wanted to enter into union with men and women. Humanity is not an afterthought to the divine purposes but has been thought of from eternity in the Son. In this sense we can say that God has never been without humanity. For the Father has always been with the Son; and in the Son and for the Son the world was created. In Barth's terminology, Jesus is the eternally elected man.

Rahner develops these ideas further when he argues that the Incarnation is the condition of possibility of the creation and not vice versa. According to Rahner, when God expresses himself, what comes to be is Jesus of Nazareth. Jesus is the perfect self-expression of the Father in space and time. As we read in John's gospel, 'He who sees me sees the Father.' (Jn. 14:9). How then should we understand the relation between creation and Incarnation? In Rahner's view, the creation is a lesser expression of God. The creation is not a perfect self-expression because there is not an identity between creator and creature. Rahner goes on to argue that we can only understand the creation properly on the basis of and in the light of the Incarnation. The Incarnation is the goal of the creation and its condition of possibility. Because God can express himself in a perfect way, he can also express himself in a lesser way, but we must understand the lesser in terms of the greater and not vice versa. Rahner puts it this way in *Foundations of Christian Faith*:

> There can indeed always be the lesser without the greater, although the lesser is always grounded in the possibility of the greater and not vice versa. To this extent we can really say: there could be men, that is, the lesser, even if the Logos had not himself become man. But we can and have to say nevertheless: the possibility that there be men is grounded in the greater, more comprehensive and more radical possibility of God to express himself in the Logos which becomes a creature.[8]

There is one final point which we should mention in this connection. According to the classical theology of the Middle Ages, the Logos is the exemplary cause of the creation, that is, we see in the Logos what the creation is meant to be. Balthasar stresses this point, for we see here the intrinsic bond between procession, creation and mission in trinitarian theology. We have tried to indicate how the creation is rooted in the divine processions. The Spirit holds open the space between the Father and the Son for the creation. The creation is ordered teleologically to the Son. Hence in the Son we see what the destiny of the creation is. Perhaps we could sum up this destiny in a word proposed by Bruno Forte: receptivity.[9] The Son is pure gift. The Son receives everything from the Father. His whole being is receptivity. Because the Son is an eternal letting-it-be, letting himself be gifted, the Son is also sheer response or sheer obedience (an obedience which, however, is not servile but filial). This eternal receptivity and obedience of the Son is the basis of the Son's historical mission. As Jesus says, 'I do always the things that are pleasing to him.' (Jn. 8:29). Our human destiny is to share in this filial obedience and receptivity. However, our destiny has been thwarted by sin. By sin, we have ceased to be *imago Dei* in the Son. Sin is our egoism by which we have become the exact opposite of what God is, i.e. we have become being turned in upon itself. We were created in giftedness, the true response of the creature is thus thanksgiving. But sin turned this receptivity into possessiveness. Rather than surrender to the Father in the Son we have clung to what is gift as though it were our own. Sin is our refusal to share in Christ's filial Sonship. Hence the historical mission of the Son: to reveal to sinful humanity its true destiny and to effect the return of a lost humanity to its trinitarian home.

The Trinity in Glory

It would be beyond the scope of the present work to discuss how this return to the Father is effected by Christ. This would require another treatise on soteriology. We have, however, already indicated the trinitarian implications of Christ's saving work when we discussed the trinitarian character of the paschal mystery (in Chapter IV). Here it must suffice to offer a few reflections as to the goal of God's trinitarian relations with the world. Again, to refer to the classical scheme of the Middle Ages such as that of Aquinas, one could say that the goal of creation is to be re-enfolded in the trinitarian life. Aquinas thus conceives the scheme of the *Summa Theologica* in terms of the exodus of the creation from God and its subsequent return to him. Bruno Forte has expressed a similar vision by speaking of exile and homecoming. We are now in exile, on pilgrimage, and especially because of our sinful condition we experience this exile as suffering, but through the victory of Christ and the power of his Spirit, we shall be brought back to our heavenly home, the Kingdom of the Trinity.

A key text of the New Testament in this regard is 1 Corinthians (15:20–28). In this text St Paul speaks of the order of God's saving events: first, Christ is raised from the dead. Then shall come the resurrection of the dead. Finally, Jesus will hand over his Kingdom to the Father. Paul writes:

Then comes the end, when he delivers the Kingdom to God the Father after destroying every rule and every authority and power. For he must reign until he has put all his enemies under his feet. The last enemy to be destroyed is death. For God has put all things in subjection under his feet. But when it says, 'All things are put in subjection under him,' it is plain that he is excepted who put all things under him. When all things are subjected to him, then the Son himself will also be subjected to him who put all things under him, that God may be everything to everyone.

A number of observations regarding this text are significant. First, we note the eschatological perspective. Christ's work is not yet complete. The decisive victory has been won in his death and resurrection. But there is still the powerful presence of death in our world. Christ's work will not be finished until the eschaton when he hands over the Kingdom to the Father. This vision accords with what Paul says in the Letter to the Romans: 'We know that the whole creation has been groaning in travail together until now; and not only the creation, but we ourselves, who have the first fruits of the Spirit, groan inwardly as we wait for adoption as sons, the redemption of our bodies.' (vs. 22–23).

Secondly, we see what we might call eschatological subordinationism. In the fourth century the church rejected the doctrine of Arius, which was a version of ontological subordinationism. Arius taught that the Son did not have the same divine status as the Father. The Council of Nicaea taught, on the contrary, that the Son was equal to the Father in everything, except that the Son was Son and the Father Father. Without in any way calling this into question, we might ask whether Nicaea did not overlook an important truth. According to the Bible, the Son is subordinate in terms of mission and obedience. As we have seen, he is pure receptivity. He is the one who is sent. A clear witness to this truth is Jesus's statement in the fourth gospel, 'The Father is greater than I.' (Jn. 14:28). Here, in I Corinthians (15), we see a confirmation of this truth. The Son is Lord, to be sure, but not Lord for his own sake. The Son fulfils his mission and realizes his identity as Son when he hands over the Kingdom to his Father. The Son does not in this moment become superfluous because his mission is complete. Rather the Son, in handing over the Kingdom, reveals his identity as Son and remains permanent mediator between the glorified creation and the Father.

At this point there is another argument which calls for attention. Thus far, we have concentrated on the relationship between the Father and the Son. But we have neglected the role of the Holy Spirit. Yet it is precisely here, after the resurrection and before the parousia, that the Spirit's role is most prominent. Jesus has sent his Spirit upon the church at Pentecost to carry on his work. It is through the Spirit that Jesus leads the world back to its trinitarian homeland. As Moltmann notes,[10] it is here in the post-resurrection period that we see the full personality of the Spirit. The Spirit has the mission to continue to make present the Kingdom which Jesus had announced in word and deed. It is also the Spirit which leads us to glorify the Son, to praise him and to confess him as Lord. The same Spirit drives believers to create anticipations of the Kingdom here and now, even in the time of exile. Thus the Spirit makes the power of Jesus's resurrection present, leads us to the confession of his glory and impels the creation toward the eschaton when God will be all in all.

From the point of view of God's trinitarian relations with the world, we see a continuing involvement of the three divine persons in the creation and in history. However, as Moltmann points out,[11] the order of relationships is not always the same. Moltmann speaks of God's searching love and his gathering love. In his eternal openness to the world, God sends his Spirit to prepare the creation for the sending of the Son. After the resurrection the Son sends the Spirit, so that the Spirit can gather up the redeemed creation into its trinitarian homeland. Here we might try to clarify how we should understand this trinitarian goal of history. Verse 28 of chapter 15 of the First Letter to the Corinthians tells us that in the eschaton God will be all in all, that God will be in his creation and that the creation will be in him. The creation will be totally penetrated by the glory of the triune God. God and the creation will remain distinct but they will interpenetrate one another. Perhaps we could say that just as classical theology spoke of the *perichoresis* of the three divine persons, so we could speak of the perichoresis of the Trinity and the creation. Admittedly it is difficult to conceive how this could be but we can get some idea of it from our human experience and from our present experience of faith. Even in human experience, in the experience of love, we get some glimpse of how two persons become one reality, are so united in love that one cannot exist without the other. This is also the experience of our faith in Christ. In Galatians (2:20), Paul says, 'I live now, not I, but Christ lives in me.' Paul's experience is that his human personality has been replaced or better transfigured by the presence of Christ in him. As he says in the same letter (Gal. 4:6), 'because we have the Spirit of Christ dwelling within us, we can call out in sonship with Christ: "Abba, Father".' Hence Paul's faith experience is that of a living *perichoresis* between Christ and himself via the Spirit of Christ who dwells within him. And this is exactly what Christ promises and prays for in the high-priestly prayer of John 17. According to St John, this is the hour of Jesus's exaltation in which Jesus prays to be glorified. But it is not an egocentric glorification. Jesus's glorification is rendered complete when he is glorified in his disciples. Jesus's glorification consists in his union with the Father. The hour of his death is the supreme manifestation of his glory, for it is his supreme surrender to the Father's will in obedience. This unity which he shares with his Father is from henceforth made available to the disciples as they are incorporated into the unity between the Father and the Son. Jesus says, 'The glory which Thou hast given me I have given to them, that they may be one even as we are one, I in them, Thou in me.' (Jn. 17:22–23). In this present experience of mutual indwelling, the depths of which are attested to by the saints and mystics, we can get a present foreshadowing of what Paul means when he says that the goal of creation is the mutual indwelling of God and the creation, in which God will be all in all.

Perhaps it would be worth nothing that this perspective allows us to see that the ultimate goal of theology is doxology and adoration. In Chapter VIII we saw that faith in the triune God has serious implications for Christian living and praxis. But it would be a mistake to believe that the ultimate goal of faith in God is action. The ultimate goal of trinitarian theology is praise. This point was made long ago by the Cappadocians with their stress on the ineffability of God, the divine darkness and the incomprehensibility of the divine processions. According to the Cappadocians, theology ought not to culminate in trinitarian definitions but in silence and adoration before the Mystery. Perhaps today we are in a similar danger. In our preoccupation with success, results and pragmatism, we are inclined to ask what is the cash value of believing in God. Against this functionalism, Moltmann rightly warns us:

> In doxology the thanks of the receiver return from the goodly gift to the giver. But the giver is not thanked merely for the sake of his good gift; he is also extolled because he himself is good. So God is not loved, worshipped and perceived merely because of the salvation that has been experienced, but for his own sake. That is to say, praise goes beyond thanksgiving. God is recognized, not only in his goodly works, but in his goodness itself. And adoration, finally, goes beyond both thanksgiving and praise. It is totally absorbed into its counterpart, in the way that we are totally absorbed by astonishment and boundless wonder. God is ultimately worshipped and loved for himself, not merely for salvation's sake.[12]

The message here is simply this. The Christian God is not a God of the gaps. God does not have a functional use. As Augustine said long ago, the good of faith is the enjoyment of God for his own sake. In this sense, we can agree with Eberhard Jüngel when he writes that God is not necessary, for necessity is defined in terms of functionality.[13] This, however, does not render God less important but more so, for as Jüngel puts it, God is more than necessary, he is interesting for his own sake. The creation, when it reaches its goal, will consequently have an eternity to explore this Mystery whose riches can never be fathomed.

Being and Becoming in God

Underlying all the discussions of this book, there has been implicitly the theme of the divine becoming. This was evident from Chapter I in which we discussed the conundrum which results from the choice between theism and atheism. A weak type of philosophical theism is adequate neither to the biblical witness nor to our contemporary human questioning. According to such an account of God, God is distant from the world and untouched by its sufferings. The world can make no difference to such a God. This theistic God has little to offer to the massive suffering which contemporary men and women endure. Nor does this type of theism correspond to the biblical vision of God who enters into history, becomes incarnate and dies on the cross. On the other hand, as we have seen, a becoming God such as that offered by process theologians and Hegelians, is a needy God. God needs the world to realize himself. God and the world are part of an all-embracing system. This version of God sacrifices the divine transcendence. In the light of this problematic and in terms of the reflections which we have pursued in this study, what answer can we give to this question? I would like to offer a response in terms of two of our leading contemporary theologians, Eberhard Jüngel and Hans Urs von Balthasar.[14]

Jüngel admits that the decisive test of Christian language about God is its ability to speak about God's historicity. This is the point which distinguishes the Christian experience of God from other conceptions of God in the ancient world. On the one hand, it is true that God by very definition is not a piece of the world. God is not an object. In this sense God by definition is radically transcendent. But Christian faith is rooted in the paschal mystery. Here we see, in the light of the resurrection, that God has identified himself with the life and death of Jesus of Nazareth. Here is the scandal for all our thinking about God; God has identified himself with a temporal event and indeed with perishability. The Incarnation and the paschal mystery challenge us to think the union of God's being with historicality.

Jüngel develops this line of reflection further, arguing that the event of God's revelation in Christ is the event of God's coming. God, in his own being, is transcendent and beyond the world. But God *comes* to the world in Jesus Christ. If there really is an identification between God and his revelation, then we must say: God's being is in coming. In other words, we cannot think of God's being as static or without movement. God's being is an eternal coming, a coming which becomes an *event* in the Incarnation and paschal mystery of Jesus.

Let us elucidate this conception in two steps. First of all, Jüngel argues that we can only do justice to the event of revelation in a trinitarian interpretation of God's being. If God has revealed himself in Jesus, then God has defined himself in him. We cannot think of God apart from this historical event, Jesus Christ. Jesus Christ belongs to the eternal being of God. God and time must be thought together. Further reflection reveals that a bare monotheism will not do to interpret this event, for the event of revelation reveals an identification between the Father and the Son. God must be defined in terms of this identification, which at the same time presupposes a differentiation. As Jüngel says, to identify with another presupposes the capacity to differentiate oneself. Hence we cannot speak of God in an undifferentiated way. We must speak of God as the relation of Father and Son. Here Jüngel can pick up Richard of St Victor's idea of God as love. If, on the basis of the cross-event, we must say that God is love, we must distinguish the lover and the beloved. Love requires a dialogue of two persons. At the same time, this love presupposes the *condilectus*, the Holy Spirit, who is the bond of union who preserves the unity of Father and Son even in the moment of their extreme separation on the cross.

Jüngel, then, like Moltmann and Balthasar, develops his trinitarian theology on the basis of the paschal mystery. He recognizes that the doctrine of the Trinity is the most difficult of all Christian affirmations, but he argues that it is indispensable to do justice to God's identification of himself with the cross of Christ. For Jüngel, the doctrine of the Trinity is the hermeneutical key to unlock the mystery of the cross as the mystery of God. Only through the doctrine of the Trinity can the story of the cross and resurrection of Jesus be told in a responsible way.

But let us pursue this reflection further in a second step to bring out more clearly the temporal or historical dimension of God's being. Jüngel formulates God's historical character in three theses: first, God comes from God. God is his own origin. God is also the origin of the revelation event. God as origin is what we mean when we speak of God as Father. Secondly, God comes to God. The goal of the revelation is also God, God the Son. God wants to come to the world, God wants to come to humankind. But how can God come to humanity without ceasing to be God? How can God come to man without making man the constitutive term of his relation and so surrendering his transcendence and the gratuity of his self-gift? This is the problem we saw posed by Knauer (in Chapter II). Jüngel's solution is substantially the same as Knauer's. God comes to the world by coming to himself. God comes to the world through the Incarnation. In Barthian language, God's coming to us in time is a repetition of his coming to himself in eternity. Because God does not want to come to himself without coming to us, there results the *event* of the Incarnation. God's decision to be himself is his decision to be for us. The immanent Trinity is the ground of the economic Trinity. God's coming to himself is the foundation of his coming to us.

But finally there is the third thesis that God comes to himself *as* God. God does not leave himself or cease to be himself when he comes to us. In the event of the cross, God does not take leave of himself. There is separation to be sure, but this separation is bridged over by God. The separation of God from himself in the cross is embraced within an ever greater union. The bond of love, is, as we have seen, the Holy Spirit. Because of the Holy Spirit as *vinculum amoris*, we can and must say that there is movement in God without alienation.

In terms of God's temporality, the Holy Spirit means that the event of God's coming is an open-ended event. In Jüngel's words, God is his own future. God is always young. The event of God's revelation, being rooted in God's being as coming, can never be overtaken. God is an inexhaustible fecundity. As Jüngel puts it, 'The concept of the trinitarian God who is love implies the eternal newness according to which the eternal Lord is always his own future. God and love never grow old. Their being is and remains one that is coming.'[15]

To sum up the doctrine, one can say with classical theology that God is Being itself. God's being is not a becoming because there is no lack in God. God's relation to the world through creation and redemption is pure gratuity. Nonetheless God's being must be understood as movement, as a coming, from God, to God, as God, that is, the eternal movement of the Father to the Son in the Holy Spirit. This eternal movement or coming grounds God's coming to us, so that Christian faith dares to say that God's being is historical. In the free, gratuitous act of revelation, God's being has become the *event* of our salvation.

To conclude these reflections, let us turn to the thought of Hans Urs von Balthasar. At the end of *Theodramatik*, Balthasar poses the question that haunts any attempt to understand the relation of God and the world: what does God receive from the world? Process theology replies that God is enriched aesthetically by his creation.

God can truly be increased by the world. Theism seems to say that God can receive nothing from the world, which in turn implies that all inner-worldly values and activities are ultimately worthless, since they contribute nothing to the supreme and everlasting reality. Balthasar seeks a solution along trinitarian lines. Again, we can develop his insights in two steps.

First, Balthasar reflects on the divine being itself. Here human language reaches its furthest limits and is often able to approach the truth only through paradoxes. The first paradox could be expressed by affirming that on the one hand God is not a becoming. Balthasar rejects this conception, because becoming implies poverty and need. On the other hand, in affirming that God is being, one must leave room for dynamism, life and movement. Although God is not becoming, God is, in Balthasar's words, trinitarian process. God is the process of a trinitarian event (*Geschehen*).[16] As he puts it, being and happening must be thought together.[17] To continue the paradoxical language, God is at once eternal rest and eternal movement.[18]

This movement or process must, however, be conceived in trinitarian terms. Balthasar prefers the language of love. God is the process or movement of eternal love, by which the Father eternally gives himself away to the Son, the Son eternally says Yes to the Father, and the Holy Spirit eternally proceeds from their mutual love as their ever greater fruitfulness. This circular movement of love gives rise to new paradoxes. The Father as source of the Trinity and origin of the Son has an infinite richness, so that the Son can never consume the Father's fullness. The Father's fullness is never exhausted and the Son never ceases to contemplate new dimensions of the Father's being. At the same time, the Holy Spirit, their mutual love, overflows in an endless creativity. Balthasar appeals explicitly to the analogy of human love. A genuine human love always contains a fullness which the two lovers never fully grasp. This genuine love is always open to be surprised by its own hidden dimensions. This is all the more true of the trinitarian community. God is the ever greater, the ever more, the ever new. Because of this, in the trinitarian life, God lets himself be enriched and God even lets himself be surprised. The Father lets himself be gifted by the Son's Yes and lets himself be surprised by the ever greater fruitfulness of the Spirit. In Balthasar's words, 'One must affirm that the infinitely rich God lets himself be gifted ever anew out of the riches of his freedom.'[19] In another text, he expresses the same point of view, when he affirms, 'God also desires to let himself be surprised by God in the sense of an excess fulfilment.'[20]

But if God in his infinite freedom can let himself be gifted in his inner-trinitarian life, then he can also let himself be gifted in the economy of salvation. For Balthasar, the becoming of the world is grounded in the eternal trinitarian process. *Theologia* is, as we have seen, the ground of the *oikonomia*. What takes place in the divine life has its analogy in the economy of salvation. Thus, if God can let himself be gifted in the eternal trinitarian life, and if this presupposes a certain desire to be poor,[21] the same holds true for the economy of salvation. The world does make a difference to God, but not in the sense that it adds something to God's being or increases his value (Hartshorne), but in the sense that out of the infinite possibilities of his freedom, God lets himself be participated in by some finite possibility. If God's being is the ever more and the ever new, then whatever becomes in the world is already included within the divine being. As Balthasar puts it, 'All finite possibilities of freedom are embraced within and occur within the already *realized* eternal life of love.'[22] From this infinite source of love and freedom, flow whatever created possibilities of freedom come to exist. As God lets himself be participated in by these created realities, he lets himself be enriched by them.

What then does God receive from the world? The argument of this book has been that an answer to this question cannot be found in classical philosophical theism nor in Hegelian or process visions of God. The answer must be sought in the Christian God, the God of history, who reveals himself through the cross of Christ to be pure unbounded love, the eternal love of the Father, the Son and the Holy Spirit. Let us then give the final word to Balthasar who answers our question in trinitarian terms:

> What does God have from the world? An additional gift, which the Father gives to the Son but which the Son just as much gives to the Father and the Spirit gives to both, a gift therefore, because the world, through the distinct working of the three persons, receives a share in the divine exchange of life, and because it gives back to God as a divine gift the divine which it received fom God together with the gift of its own createdness.[23]

Notes

Preface
1 Otto Hermann Pesch, *Frei Sein aus Gnade, Theologische Anthropologie* (Freiburg, Basel, Wien: Herder, 1983), p. 18.

Chapter I: The Dilemma of Contemporary Thinking About God
1 See E. Jüngel, *God as the Mystery of the World* (Edinburgh: T. and T. Clark, 1983), pp. 184ff.
2 *Summa Theologica*, I, q. 13, art. 7.
3 John Macquarrie, *Thinking about God* (London: SCM, 1975), p. 111.
4 Norris Clarke, 'A New Look at the Immutability of God' in *God Knowable and Unknowable*, edited by R. Roth (New York: Fordham University Press, 1973), p. 44.
5 A. N. Whitehead, *Process and Reality, An Essay in Cosmology* (New York: Harper and Row, 1960), p. 32.
6 *Ibid.*, p. 529.
7 *Ibid.*, p. 11.
8 *Ibid.*, pp. 343-4.
9 Peter Knauer, *Der Glaube kommt vom Hören* (Frankfurt: 1982), p. 28.
10 In presenting this interpretation of Descartes, I am following Jüngel, *op. cit.*, pp. 111ff.
11 *Ibid.*, pp. 125-6.
12 See *Ibid.*, pp. 145-50.
13 Nietzsche, *Thus Spake Zarathustra*. As cited by Jüngel, *ibid.*, p. 149.
14 See E. Jüngel, 'Keine Menschlösigkeit Gottes, Zur Theologie Karl Barths zwischen Theismus und Atheismus', *Evangelische Theologie* 31 (1971), pp. 376-90.
15 See W. Kasper, *The God of Jesus Christ* (London: SCM, 1983), chapter 2, especially p. 38.
16 See Hannah Arendt, *Über die Revolution* (München: R. Piper, 1963).
17 See Kasper, *op. cit.*, pp. 46, 52ff., 106-9.
18 W. Kasper, *Jesus the Christ* (London: Burns and Oates, 1976), p. 73.
19 J. Moltmann, *The Crucified God* (London: SCM, 1974), pp. 219-20.
20 J. Moltmann, *The Experiment of Hope* (Philadelphia: Fortress Press, 1975), p. 82.
21 See M. Horkheimer, *Die Sehnsucht nach dem ganz Anderen. Ein Interview mit Kommentar von Hellmut Gumnior* (Hamburg: 1970).
22 See E. Jüngel, *God as the Mystery of the World* and J. Moltmann, *The Crucified God*.

Chapter II: Revelation and Trinity

1 DS 3015.
2 Kant, *Der Streit der Fakultäten*, Philosophische Bibliothek, Leipzig, p. 34.
3 Karl Barth, 'Revelation'. In *Revelation: A Symposium*, edited by John Baillie and H. Martin (London: 1937), p. 42.
4 *Ibid.*, p. 45.
5 *Ibid.*, p. 46.
6 Moltmann criticizes Barth at this point, for Moltmann believes that one cannot import into theology an alien concept of Lordship. Rather than develop the doctrine of the Trinity in terms of an *a priori* concept of Lordship, Moltmann argues that we must develop the understanding of Lordship on the basis of God's trinitarian history. See *The Trinity and the Kingdom of God* (London: SCM, 1981), pp. 139–44.
7 Karl Barth, *Church Dogmatics* I (Edinburgh: T. and T. Clark, 1975), p. 476.
8 Peter Knauer, *Der Glaube kommt vom Hören* (Frankfurt am Main: 1982), p. 75.
9 *Ibid.*, pp. 103–4.
10 *Ibid.*, p. 104.
11 Karl Rahner, *Foundations of Christian Faith* (London: Darton, Longman and Todd, 1978), p. 170.
12 *Ibid.*, p. 69.
13 *Ibid.*, p. 64.
14 *Ibid.*, p. 62.
15 Karl Rahner, 'Current Problems in Christology', *Theological Investigations* I (London: Darton, Longman and Todd, 1974), p. 181.
16 *Ibid.*, p. 191.
17 Karl Rahner, 'The Theology of the Symbol'. In *Theological Investigations* IV (London: Darton, Longman and Todd, 1966), p. 237.
18 *Foundations of Christian Faith*, p. 290.
19 *Ibid.*, p. 128.
20 *Ibid.*, p. 137.
21 Meyendorff, *Introduction a l'étude de Gregoire Palamas* (Paris: 1959), p. 298.
22 Karl Barth, *Church Dogmatics* I, p. 479.
23 Walter Kasper, *The God of Jesus Christ* (London: SCM, 1983), p. 270.
24 *Ibid.*, pp. 273–7.
25 Rahner, *Foundations of Christian Faith*, p. 220.
26 *Ibid.*, pp. 220–1.
27 See Kasper, *op. cit.*, p. 276.

Chapter III: Jesus, the Son and Bearer of the Spirit

1 E. Jüngel, *God as the Mystery of the World* (Edinburgh: T. and T. Clark, 1983), pp. 351–2, note 22.

2 Robert Butterworth, 'The Doctrine of the Trinity', *The Way* 24 (1984), p. 54.

3 Martin Hengel, *The Son of God* (London: SCM, 1976), p. 63.

4 C. F. D. Moule, *The Origin of Christology* (Cambridge University Press: 1977), pp. 30–1.

5 Reginald Fuller, *The Foundations of New Testament Christology* (New York: Charles Scribner's Sons, 1965), p. 130.

6 James Dunn, *Jesus and the Spirit: A Study of the Religious and Charismatic Experience of Jesus and the First Christians as Reflected in the New Testament* (London: SCM, 1975), p. 39.

7 Edward Schillebeeckx, *Jesus, An Experiment in Christology* (London: Collins, 1979) p. 269.

8 *Ibid.*, p. 260.

9 *Ibid.*, p. 263.

10 Raymond Brown, unpublished lecture, 'The Christology of the New Testament'. See also *Jesus, God and Man* (Milwaukee: Bruce Publishing Co., 1967), pp. 88–9. Fr Brown is drawing on the scholarship of Joachim Jeremias. See Jeremias, *New Testament Theology* (London: SCM, 1965), pp. 61–8; also *The Central Message of the New Testament* (London: SCM, 1965), pp. 9–30.

11 James Dunn, *op. cit.*, pp. 53–62.

12 *Ibid.*, p. 60.

13 *Ibid.*, p. 67.

14 Heribert Mühlen, 'Das Christusereignis als Tat des Heiligen Geistes'. In *Mysterium Salutis* 3/2, edited by J. Feiner and M. Löhrer (Einsiedeln: 1969), p. 522.

15 Moule, *op. cit.*, pp. 29–30.

16 *Ibid.*, p. 18.

17 *Ibid.*, p. 27.

Chapter IV: Trinity and the Paschal Mystery

1 Jon Sobrino, *Christology at the Crossroads* (London: SCM, 1978), p. 105.

2 *Ibid.*, p. 94.

3 See Moltmann, *The Crucified God* (London: SCM, 1974), chapter 4.

4 E. Peterson, *Der Monotheismus als politisches Problem* (Leipzig: Hegner, 1935.

5 L. Keck, *A Future for the Historical Jesus* (Nashville: Abingdon Press, 1971), p. 229.

6 *Ibid.*, p. 231.

7 See Moltmann, *op. cit.*, pp. 241ff.

8 *Ibid.*

9 See Moltmann, *ibid.*, p. 241; Hans Urs von Balthasar, *Mysterium Paschale*, in *Mysterium Salutis*, III, 2 edited by J. Feiner and M. Löhrer (Einsiedeln: Benziger, 1969), pp. 198ff.

10 For the development of this point, see von Balthasar, *Christlicher Stand* (Einsiedeln: Johannes, 1977), pp. 148f.; also *The von Balthasar Reader*, edited by Medard Kehl and Werner Löser (Edinburgh: T. and T. Clark, 1982), p. 179.

11 See von Balthasar, *Theodramatik* III (Einsiedeln: Johannes, 1980), pp. 297–305; also *Herrlichkeit* III, 2, Teil 2 (Einsiedeln: Johannes, 1969), p. 208.

12 *Theodramatik* III, p. 304.

13 *Ibid.*, p. 302.

14 See especially *Mysterium Paschale* in *Mysterium Salutis* III, 2, pp. 227–55.

15 *The von Balthasar Reader*, p. 153.

16 See Norbert Hoffmann, *Kreuz und Trinität, Zur Theologie der Sühne* (Einsiedeln: Johannes, 1982).

17 *Ibid.*, p. 31.

18 For the development of this point, see Pope John Paul II, Encyclical Letter *Dominum et Vivicantem*, no. 40.

19 J. Moltmann, *The Future of Creation* (London: SCM, 1979), p. 73.

Chapter V: God and the Holy Spirit

1 Vladimir Lossky, *The Mystical Theology of the Eastern Church* (Crestwood, NY.: St Vladimir's Seminary Press, 1976), p. 244.

2 *Ibid.*, pp. 162–4.

3 *Ad Serapion* I, 23 as cited by C. Vagaggini, *Theological Dimensions of the Liturgy* (Collegeville, Minn.: The Liturgical Press, 1976), p. 205.

4 *De Trin.*, Bk. XV, ch. 18, no. 32.

5 Karl Rahner, *Foundations of Christian Faith* (London: Darton, Longman and Todd, 1978), p. 125.

6 *Ibid.*, p. 121.

7 Kilian McDonnell, 'A Trinitarian Theology of the Holy Spirit', *Theological Studies* 46, 2 (1985), p. 223.

8 *De Trin.*, Bk. VIII, ch. 10, no. 14.

9 *Ibid.*, Bk. V, ch. 11, no. 12.

10 Jürgen Moltmann, *The Church in the Power of the Spirit* (London: SCM, 1977), pp. 55–6.

11 Walter Kasper, *The God of Jesus Christ* (London: SCM, 1984), p. 226.

12 See Heribert Mühlen, *Der Heilige Geist als Person* (Münster: 1966). Also Hans Urs von Balthasar, 'Der Unbekannte Jenseits des Wortes', in *Spiritus Creator* (Einsiedeln: Johannes, 1967), pp. 95–105; 'Der Heilige Geist als Liebe', *ibid.*, pp. 106–22.

13 Philip Rosato, 'Spirit Christology: Ambiguity and Promise', *Theological Studies* 38 (1977), pp. 423–49.

14 See Walter Kasper, Jesus the Christ (London: Burns and Oates, 1976), pp. 252ff.

15 See Hans Urs von Balthasar, *Pneuma und Institution* (Einsiedeln: Johannes, 1974), p. 224.

16 See Rosato, *art. cit.*, p. 445.

17 Jürgen Moltmann, *The Trinity and the Kingdom of God* (London: SCM, 1981), p. 94.

18 *Lumen Gentium*, no. 8.

19 Heribert Mühlen, *Una Mystica Persona* (München, Paderborn, Wien: Verlag Ferdinand Schöningh, 1967).

20 Lossky, *op. cit.*, pp. 167–8.

21 See *ibid.*, p. 73.

22 Kasper, *The God of Jesus Christ*, p. 220.

23 Francis Sullivan, *Charisms and Charismatic Renewal* (Dublin: Gill and Macmillan, 1982), p. 13.

24 See *Pneuma und Institution*, p. 139.

25 See for example *Spiritus Creator* (Einsiedeln: Johannes, 1967), p. 443; the same idea is also stressed in *Pneuma und Institution*, p. 153.

26 See J. Ratzinger, 'Bemerkungen zur Frage der Charismen in der Kirche', in *Die Zeit Jesu, Festschrift für Heinrich Schlier* (Freiburg, Basel, Wien: Herder, 1970).

27 *Pneuma und Institution*, p. 226.

28 See Medard Kehl, *Kirche als Institution* (Frankfurt: J. Knecht, 1976), p. 278.

29 Yves Congar, *I Believe in the Holy Spirit*, Volume 3 (London: Chapman, 1983), p. 201.

30 Kasper, *The God of Jesus Christ*, pp. 218–19.

31 Congar, *op. cit.*, p. 40.

32 See Lossky, *op. cit.*, ch. 2, 'The Divine Darkness', pp. 23–43.

33 *De fede orth.* I,7 as cited by Kasper, *The God of Jesus Christ*, p. 217.

34 *De Trin.* Bk. XV, ch. 17, no. 29.

35 DS 850.

36 Kasper, *The God of Jesus Christ*, p. 222.

37 See *The Trinity and the Kingdom of God*, pp. 178–90.

38 *Ibid.*, p. 185.

39 See Jürgen Moltmann and Elizabeth Wendel-Moltmann, *Humanity in God* (London: SCM, 1983), p. 89.

40 See Donald Gelpi, *The Divine Mother, A Trinitarian Theology of the Holy Spirit* (Lanham, Md.: University of America Press, 1984).

41 Congar, *op. cit.*, p. 157.

42 See *ibid.*, p. 159.

43 As we have seen, Hans Urs von Balthasar develops this point extensively in his theology. See my essay 'Man and Woman as Imago Dei in the Theology of Hans Urs von Balthasar', in *Clergy Review* LXVIII (1983), pp. 117–28.

Chapter VI: The Concept of Person in Trinitarian Theology

1 Augustine, *De Trinitate*, Book V, 9.

2 Josef Ratzinger, *Dogma e Predicazione* (Brescia: Queriniana, 1974), p. 183.

3 Richard of St Victor, *De Trinitate*, IV, 22, 24.

4 For Mühlen's appropriation of Richard of St Victor, see *Der Heilige Geist als Person* (Münster: 1966).

5 *Summa Theologica* I, q. 29, art. 1.

6 Jürgen Moltmann, *Trinity and the Kingdom of God* (London: SCM, 1981), p. 190.

7 Karl Barth, *Church Dogmatics* I (Edinburgh: T. and T. Clark, 1975), p. 359.

8 Karl Rahner, *The Trinity* (London: Herder, 1970), p. 109.

9 Ratzinger, *op. cit.*, p. 188.

10 Moltmann, *op. cit.*, 145.

11 *Ibid.*, pp. 143–4; 192–200.

12 Joseph Bracken, 'The Holy Trinity as a Community of Divine Persons', *Heythrop Journal* 15 (1974), pp. 166–82; 257–70.

13 Bracken, *The Triune Symbol: Persons, Process and Community* (Lanham, Md.: University of America Press, 1985), p. 7.

14 Bracken, *art. cit.*, p. 180.

15 Bracken, *op. cit.*, p. 26.

16 In addition to *Trinity and the Kingdom of God*, see, for example, the book which he authored in partnership with his wife: *Humanity in God* (London: SCM, 1983).

17 Moltmann, *Humanity in God*, p. 104.

18 William Hill, *The Three-Personed God, the Trinity as a Mystery of Salvation* (Washington, DC: The Catholic University of America Press, 1982), p. 255.

19 *Ibid.*, p. 272.

20 Walter Kasper, *The God of Jesus Christ* (London: SCM, 1984), p. 289.

21 François Bourassa, 'Personne et Conscience en theologie trinitaire', *Gregorianum* LV (1974), p. 709.

Chapter VII: Analogy of Being and Analogy of Faith

1 Karl Barth, *Church Dogmatics*, vol. 1 (Edinburgh: T. and T. Clark, 1975), p. 392.

2 For Balthasar's interpretation of Barth, see Hans Urs von Balthasar, *Karl Barth, Darstellung und Deutung seiner Theologie* (Einsiedeln: Johannes Verlay, 1976). An abbreviated version was published in English with the title, *The Theology of Karl Barth* (New York: 1971).

3 For what follows see W. Norris Clarke, 'The Metaphysical Ascent to God through Participation and the Analogical Structure of our Language about God', in *A Philosophical Approach to God* (Winston-Salem, North Carolina: Wake Forest University, 1979), pp. 33–65.

4 *Ibid.*, p. 40.

5 See Eberhard Jüngel, *God as the Mystery of the World* (Edinburgh: T. and T. Clark, 1983), pp. 363–4.

6 See *ibid.*, pp. 258–60, 296–7.

7 See Eberhard Jüngel, 'Metaphorische Wahrheit. Erwägungen zur theologischen Relevanz der Metapher als Beitrag zur Hermeneutik einer narrativen Theologie', in *Entsprechungen: God–Wahrheit–Mensch* (München: Kaiser, 1980), p. 149.

8 For this example, I am indebted to Leander Keck, *A Future for the Historical Jesus* (Nashville, Tenn.: Abingdon Press, 1971), p. 248.

9 See John Dominic Crossan, *The Dark Interval, Towards a Theology of Story* (Argus Communications: 1975).

10 *Ibid.*, p. 57.

11 See *ibid.*, pp. 123–128; Jüngel, *God as the Mystery of the World*, p. 288; L. Keck, *A Future for the Historical Jesus*, pp. 243–9.

12 George de Schrijver develops this aspect of Balthasar's theology in his *Le Merveilleux Accord de L'Homme et de Dieu, Étude de L'Analogie de L'Être chez Hans Urs von Balthasar* (Leuven University Press: 1983).

13 Walter Kasper, *The God of Jesus Christ* (London: SCM, 1983), pp. 94–9.

14 *Ibid.*, p. 99.

15 Jürgen Moltmann, *The Crucified God* (London: SCM, 1974), pp. 27–8

Chapter VIII: Trinitarian Faith and Praxis

1 Kant, *Der Streit der Fakultäten* (Philosophische Bibliothek, Leipzig, 252), p. 34, as cited by J. Moltmann, *The Trinity and the Kingdom of God* (London: SCM, 1981), p. 6.

2 See Matthew Lamb, 'The Theory–Praxis Relationship in Contempor-

ary Christian Theologies', *Proceedings of the Catholic Theological Society of America* 31 (1976), pp. 149–78. See also Charles Davis, 'Theology and Praxis', *Cross Currents* (Summer, 1973), pp. 154–68.

3 J. B. Metz, *Faith in History and Society* (London: Burns and Oates, 1980), p. 165.

4 See John C. Haughey, 'Jesus as the Justice of God', in *The Faith that Does Justice* edited by John C. Haughey (New York: Paulist Press, 1977), pp. 264–90.

5 John R. Donahue, 'Biblical Perspectives on Justice', in *The Faith that Does Justice*, p. 69.

6 José Míguez Bonino, *Toward a Christian Political Ethics* (Philadelphia: Fortress Press, 1983), p. 85.

7 *Ibid.*, p. 98.

8 See Dermot Lane, *Foundations for a Social Theology, Praxis, Process and Salvation* (Dublin: Gill and Macmillan, 1984), p. 81.

9 *Instruction on Christian Freedom and Liberation*, Congregation for the Doctrine of the Faith, 22 March 1986, no. 60.

10 See J. Moltmann, *On Human Dignity, Political Theology and Ethics* (London: SCM, 1984), pp. 100ff.

11 *Ibid.*, p. 109.

12 *Ibid.*, p. 102.

13 For the development of this point, see Roger Haight, *An Alternative Vision, An Intrepretation of Liberation Theology* (New York: Paulist Press, 1985), pp. 25ff.

14 *Ibid.*, p. 42.

15 Jon Sobrino, *Christology at the Crossroads* (London: SCM, 1978), p. 392.

16 E. Peterson, *Monotheismus als Politisches Problem* (Leipzig: Hegner, 1935).

17 See J. Moltmann, *The Crucified God* (London: SCM, 1974), pp. 325ff.; *The Trinity and the Kingdom of God*, pp. 129ff., 197ff.

18 See the critique of G. Ruggieri in the introduction to the Italian edition of Peterson's study, *Il monoteismo come problema politico*, edited by G. Ruggieri (Brescia: Queriniana, 1983), p. 21.

19 Moltmann, *The Trinity and the Kingdom of God*, pp. 197–8.

20 John Donahue, 'The Parable of the Sheep and the Goats: A Challenge to Christian Ethics', *Theological Studies* 47 (March 1986), p. 24.

21 In addition to Donahue, Moltmann stresses the christological character of the parable. See *The Church in the Power of the Spirit* (London: SCM, 1977), pp. 126–30.

22 Donahue, 'Biblical Perspectives on Justice', in *The Faith that Does Justice*, p. 105.

23 See Donahue, 'The Parable of the Sheep and the Goats: A Challenge to Christian Ethics', pp. 25ff.

24 Dorr uses this term to describe the vision of Pope John Paul II. See Donal Dorr, *Option for the Poor, a Hundred Years of Vatican Social Teaching* (Dublin: Gill and Macmillan, 1983), p. 260.

25 One could mention such thinkers as Ebner, Rosenzweig, Buber and George Herbert Mead. Pannenberg's *Anthropology in Theological Perspective* (Edinburgh: T. and T. Clark, 1985) has considered the social constitution of the self in great detail. See also Berhard Casper, *Das Dialogische Denken, Eine Untersuchung der religionsphilosophischen Bedeutung Franz Rosenzweigs, Ferdinand Ebners und Martin Bubers* (Freiburg, Basel, Wien: Herder, 1967).

26 J. B. Metz, *op. cit.*, p. 73.

27 Moltmann, *The Trinity and the Kingdom of God*, p. 216.

28 Dorr, *op. cit.*, p. 245.

29 Haight, *op. cit.*, p. 79.

30 *Instruction on Christian Freedom and Liberation*, no. 57.

Chapter IX: Trinitarian Prayer

1 See Hans Urs von Balthasar, *Prayer* (London: Geoffrey Chapman, 1961), ch. II.

2 Hans Urs von Balthasar, *Christlich Meditieren* (Herder: Freiburg, 1984), p. 7.

3 Karl Rahner, 'The Eternal Significance of the Humanity of Jesus for our Relationship to God', *Theological Investigations* III (London: Darton, Longman and Todd, 1974), pp. 35–46.

4 See Karl Barth, *Church Dogmatics* I,1 (Edinburgh: T. and T. Clark, 1975), no. 4.

5 *Dei Verbum*, no. 25.

6 *Ibid.*, no. 21.

7 Balthasar, *Prayer*, p. 66.

8 Franz Jalics, *Lernen Wir Beten* (München: Verlag J. Pfeiffer, 1981).

9 See, for example, Kallistos Ware and Emmanuel Jungclaussen, *The Power of the Name* (SLG Press, Convent of the Incarnation, Fairacres, Oxford, 1982); M. Basil Pennington, *Centering Prayer* (Doubleday, Image Book, 1982); John Main, *Word into Silence* (London: Darton, Longman and Todd, 1980); William Johnston, *The Mysticism of the Cloud of Unknowing* (St Meinrad, Indiana: Abbey Press, 1957).

10 Walter Kasper, *The God of Jesus Christ* (London: SCM, 1984), pp. 305f.

11 Pennington, *op. cit.*, p. 127.

12 *Presbyterorum Ordinis*, no. 5, 3.

13 Cyprian Vagaggini, *Theological Dimensions of the Liturgy* (Collegeville, Minn.: The Liturgical Press, 1976), pp. 223–4.

14 Yves Congar, *I Believe in the Holy Spirit*, Vol. III (London: Geoffrey Chapman, 1983), p. 264.

15 *De Trin*. III, 4, 10 (PL 42, 874) as cited by Congar, *ibid*., p. 251.

16 Augustine, *Tract. in Ioan*., XXVII, 11.

17 Louis Bouyer, *Eucharist*, translated by C. V. Quinn from the second French edition (Notre Dame, 1968), p. 467.

Chapter X: God and World in Trinitarian Perspective

1 Walter Kasper, *The God of Jesus Christ* (London: SCM, 1983), p. 295.

2 Hans Urs von Balthasar, *Theodramatik* II, 1 (Einsiedeln: Johannes, 1978), p. 262.

3 Bonaventure as cited by Balthasar, *Theodramatik* IV (Einsiedeln: Johannes, 1983), p. 56, *n*. 13.

4 Thomas Aquinas as cited in *ibid*., p. 53, note 2.

5 See *ibid*., p. 53.

6 Adrienne von Speyr as cited by J. Moltmann, *The Church in the Power of the Spirit* (London: SCM, 1977), p. 60.

7 Balthasar, *Theodramatik* IV, pp. 387–8.

8 Karl Rahner, *Foundations of Christian Faith* (London: Darton, Longman and Todd, 1978), p. 223.

9 See Bruno Forte, *Trinità come storia* (Paoline, 1985), p. 163.

10 J. Moltmann, *The Trinity and the Kingdom of God* (London: SCM, 1981), pp. 125–6.

11 *Ibid*., p. 127.

12 *Ibid*., p. 153.

13 Eberhard Jüngel, *God as the Mystery of the World* (Edinburgh: T. and T. Clark, 1983), pp. 24ff.

14 These ideas are developed principally in Jüngel's *God as the Mystery of the World* and Balthasar's *Theodramatik* IV.

15 Jüngel, *op. cit.*, p. 375.

16 Balthasar, *Theodramatik* IV, pp. 66–7.

17 *Ibid*., p. 59.

18 *Ibid*., p. 67.

19 *Ibid*., p. 465.

20 *Ibid*., p. 69, note 54.

21 *Ibid*., p. 465.

22 *Ibid*.

23 *Ibid*., p. 476.

Index of Names